CW00726234

CAMBRIDGE LIBRARY

Books of enduring schola

Botany and Horticulture

Until the nineteenth century, the investigation of natural phenomena, plants and animals was considered either the preserve of elite scholars or a pastime for the leisured upper classes. As increasing academic rigour and systematisation was brought to the study of 'natural history', its subdisciplines were adopted into university curricula, and learned societies (such as the Royal Horticultural Society, founded in 1804) were established to support research in these areas. A related development was strong enthusiasm for exotic garden plants, which resulted in plant collecting expeditions to every corner of the globe, sometimes with tragic consequences. This series includes accounts of some of those expeditions, detailed reference works on the flora of different regions, and practical advice for amateur and professional gardeners.

The Garden of Ignorance

Marion Cran (1875–1942), born in South Africa, passed most of her life in England, and, from 1910 until her death, lived and gardened in a house called 'Coggers' near Benenden in Kent. She was a prolific writer of books and articles on gardening, and was the first radio broadcaster on gardening in Britain. This 1913 work combines prescriptive gardening advice with autobiography: she admits that, although she had longed to live in the country, 'I knew nothing at all of gardening; never did anyone know less.' When she first arrived at the 'rented three shaggy acres of ground in Surrey' in which she made her first garden, it took her some time to decide to tame the wilderness. In an entertaining narrative, she describes her journey from ignorance of plants themselves, soil types and manures, planting aspects and pruning regimes, to hands-on expertise and wild enthusiasm.

Cambridge University Press has long been a pioneer in the reissuing of out-of-print titles from its own backlist, producing digital reprints of books that are still sought after by scholars and students but could not be reprinted economically using traditional technology. The Cambridge Library Collection extends this activity to a wider range of books which are still of importance to researchers and professionals, either for the source material they contain, or as landmarks in the history of their academic discipline.

Drawing from the world-renowned collections in the Cambridge University Library and other partner libraries, and guided by the advice of experts in each subject area, Cambridge University Press is using state-of-the-art scanning machines in its own Printing House to capture the content of each book selected for inclusion. The files are processed to give a consistently clear, crisp image, and the books finished to the high quality standard for which the Press is recognised around the world. The latest print-on-demand technology ensures that the books will remain available indefinitely, and that orders for single or multiple copies can quickly be supplied.

The Cambridge Library Collection brings back to life books of enduring scholarly value (including out-of-copyright works originally issued by other publishers) across a wide range of disciplines in the humanities and social sciences and in science and technology.

The Garden of Ignorance

Ignorance

The Experiences of a Woman in a Garden

M ARION C RAN

CAMBRIDGE
UNIVERSITY PRESS

CAMBRIDGE
UNIVERSITY PRESS

University Printing House, Cambridge, CB2 8BS, United Kingdom

Cambridge University Press is part of the University of Cambridge.
It furthers the University's mission by disseminating knowledge in the pursuit of
education, learning and research at the highest international levels of excellence.

www.cambridge.org
Information on this title: www.cambridge.org/9781108076593

© in this compilation Cambridge University Press 2017

This edition first published 1913
This digitally printed version 2017

ISBN 978-1-108-07659-3 Paperback

THE
GARDEN
OF
IGNORANCE

A SUN-BATH IN THE GARDEN OF DREAMS-COME-TRUE

THE GARDEN OF IGNORANCE

THE EXPERIENCES OF A WOMAN IN A GARDEN

BY
MRS.
GEORGE
CRAN
F.R.H.S.

WITH TWENTY-NINE
ILLUSTRATIONS

HERBERT JENKINS LIMITED
ARUNDEL PLACE HAYMARKET
LONDON S.W. ❧ ❧ MCMXIII

THE ANCHOR PRESS, LTD., TIPTREE, ESSEX

TO
MY FATHER

CONTENTS

ILLUSTRATIONS

ILLUSTRATIONS

THE
GARDEN
OF
IGNORANCE

THE GARDEN OF IGNORANCE

CHAPTER I

ON GARDENS

LOVAT said to his wife one day, " Flowers ! You don't know the beginning of the meaning of flowers ! When *I* see them they make a lump in my throat." Now Lovat is ordinary enough to look at ; by that I mean he is good-looking, young, with the alert hard look of the man of affairs, who wrenches from the world of men a living for him and his. To look at him, swart, vigorous, practical,—comfortable too, a little,—one would hardly suspect him of harbouring a heart susceptible to the still small voices of nature. Indeed, one would sooner suspect his wife, with her wonderful eyes like calm after storm, yet she is utterly and entirely deaf to all call of the country, and lives as completely social a life as anyone I know.

B

People are very interesting. I sometimes feel as though I were passing my days in a huge bazaar where is an inexhaustible bran pie. I dip in, and dip in, dragging out now and again a bag of blood and nerve and muscle which is a new friendship; and slowly through the days unwrap the parcel to find what is hidden inside. The oddest shaped parcels frequently contain the nicest insides. I found one at a poker party once; a burly, industrious bluffer, who became distraught and silent at the critical moment when a heavy ace-pot had just been opened. He looked as though he could not hear for listening; and it transpired that a heavy gale which was whistling and roaring round the house held him in the toils of memory and fancy. I became so interested in him that I lost pleasure in the game, for I too am liable to soul seizure when I get caught by the rough side of the tongue of a gale.

Some people have that emotional feeling towards nature, and some have not. It is impossible from externals to tell who suffers from it and who is immune—it flourishes in the most unlikely breasts, and is absent in

the most seeming likely. But I believe that
generally it is the country-born urbans who
feel it most. It is an extraordinary yearn-
ing ; a sentimental pull at the heart-strings ;
a desire akin to the need of a lover for his
mistress, a soul-sickness that leaves an intoler-
able ache. It finds expression in many ways
—of some men it makes poets ; some it
only drives to linger and look long in flower-
shop windows ; some of the very poor it
makes endure constant small sacrifices to
buy flowers for the house ; others it sends
into parks to hear the tree-sounds, to feel
grass under the feet, to look on growing
flowers ; of some it makes gardeners, of some
poachers, of some pioneers. For myself (in
the days when a garden to own was a beautiful dream beyond the wildest hope of ful-
filment) it would send me scudding past the
parks and squares with averted eyes, unable
to endure the sheen of laburnum, the tossing
guelder roses, the exquisite green of May
. . . once a blackbird sang in Chelsea gardens
on a Sunday evening, and I stood weeping
in the dusty road as utterly unable to control
the pain I felt as the bird his singing. I

could not, in those days of stress and a City life, look into the face of Nature without tears.

People are built differently. To some the sound of traffic brings pleasure, to me the hum of the honey bee ; to some the brilliant vitality of London, to me the wet wind over vasty downs ; to some Covent Garden Opera House full of cultured music and the glitter of gems, to me the brown nightingale in the valley with moon and the stars for jewels. It's a question of taste.   Opopanax or roses. Asphalt or turf.   Pose or repose.

If you want anything badly enough it will come, only you must want it with the whole heart.   That is wonderfully, graciously true of life.   I suppose why we get what we want in the end, is that if we want badly enough we never lose a single opportunity of pressing towards the dearly-desired goal. There came a magic day when the Master rented three acres of shaggy ground in Surrey and I entered into paradise.

A modern slate-tiled cottage, papered inside with the usual deadly patterns and colours at 7d. a piece, was set near a pine wood with a field below, very much off the high road. So we took the wood and field into the grounds and set to work with distemper and paint to make a cool restful home. I notice people always try to make a country cottage " cool " and the *pied-à-terre* in town " cosy " ; dirt being cosy, and cleanliness cool. The most strenuous labour of the most heaven-sent housewife ever born will not save one in London from the infiltration of an ineffable misty grey—an all-pervading indescribable yellow-grey film, which signs and seals the London homes, so that there are chosen there, wisely and well, the darker warmer colours which betray the fog fingers less readily than others ; and in the country, with a glorious reaction, cream distemper, muslin and chintz.

The Master is not sensitive to a hideous wallpaper, and I am. I need only be left long enough in company with one to become a sordid squalid mass of unresisting misery. He said the papers were clean and therefore all right. I said they were ugly and therefore all wrong. It ended in my undertaking to paint and distemper the place throughout myself. It sounds much nobler than it

really was, since the village carpenter lent
scaffolding and steps, and showed me how to
mix the distemper, which laid well over the
clean new paper ; it took three coats to each
room to obliterate the staring patterns, and
a sailor-man friend came and helped with the
giddiest parts of landings and stairs.   It took
a fair quantity of distemper to turn all those
ugly walls into a warm deep cream ;   the
wood-work we painted walnut brown.   When
arm and shoulder muscles became accustomed
to the monotonous rhythmic exercise, the
adventure became wholly joyous.   I liked
the quaint disinfectant smell of the distemper ;
it was fresh and wholesome.   I grew fond of
the magic brush that turned aggressive
designs into a peaceful monotone.   I loved
the clatter of pail and brush in the empty
echoing rooms ; and all the time I was working
I was dimly conscious of the garden outside.
With the splash of the brush went a ceaseless
accompaniment of sound like waves breaking
on a pebbly beach.   It was the sound of
wind in the pines.   I knew nothing at all
of gardening ; never did anyone know less. I
thought it meant weeding and backache. One

day I saw a man's face through the window; he had with him a rhododendron in a pot, heavily set with bud. He offered it to me for four shillings. I offered to make it five shillings if he would show me how to plant it, which he very kindly did. I may say that I have been a cherished client of his ever since, only on less hysterical terms. He brings me sloes in season, and baskets of kingcups from the marshes near Frensham, and bluebells from the wood which the White Lady haunts o' nights, and " masheroons " after heavy autumnal rains.

Having no garden tools he scrabbed a hole in the light sandy soil with his fingers and we planted the rhododendron in the wood, where I trod on it in the dark two days later and slaughtered it. As I had not begun to take gardening at all seriously, the loss of the handsome plant disturbed me less than the waste of money. What I might, had I been more keen, have interpreted as an unlucky omen for the garden, was therefore only an unfortunate incident.

One drifts unconsciously into the passions of life. I did not know as I worked happily

with pail and brush that that delicious under-
current of sound, like a breaking sea, was to
weave itself into the tissue of my days and
become so much part of life that there should
be an active agony for me ever more in missing
it—that it should tint the fabric of the years
with its own peculiar colour.   The sound of
the wind in pine trees has a sombre radiance,
penetrating, mournful, joyous, and any reader
who has suffered that sound to impinge on
his emotional life will know what I mean
when I say this.   It is nonsense to everyone
else.   As I listened and worked, unconscious
of the fetter being forged, I went wishing (in
that incompetent irritable way ignorance has
of wishing) that the ugly messy garden would
spread away into spaces of green turf, into
arches and glades and brave spots of colour.
But I never imagined making those things
for myself . . . till a guest said one day at
the gate, looking back on the untidy litter,
" What a paradise this will be after you've
worked in it two or three years."   The idea
that a garden was a canvas on which to paint
a picture in flowers and trees and winding
paths never occurred to me till that moment ;

and from that moment it has never left me. A landscape gardener was created with a sentence.

I took the hand of my wishes and led them through the overgrown wood ; over harsh hillocks of grass and gorse in the field below where a neighbouring peasant's lean pony grazed ; and round the sandy waste in front of the cottage where lone cabbages reared unsightly stalks—a very abomination of desolation—redeemed by clumps of trees, good big hedges and the acre or so of pine wood adjoining. I led those whimpering young unformed wishes round on many and many a morn and eve till they grew sturdy tiresome companions, until they clamoured for space and light, for roses, for fruit trees, for lawns, for masses and avenues of colour ; I lived with them till they peopled the place ; and the garden as it was ceased to exist. It became an imagined paradise complete, mapped out, planned, and ever-improving in my heart. What *joy* the dream-garden gave ! Long winter evenings were spent with Mr. Cook's delightfully illustrated book " Gardens of England " on my knee, the book which made me long for a dovecote and a daffodil walk ; long hours, immeasurably happy, went to the study of catalogues. My presents became the scandal of the family ; asked what I wanted for Christmas I said half a dozen loads of manure, for Easter as many of loam, for my birthday eight tons of " pitching " stones to pave the terrace—and so on till my " mania " showed such fair results that it was toned down to a " hobby " and enthusiasm was justified of her child.

Gardening speedily became a series of illuminating flashes ; it was strange to have to readjust the mental attitude with every added fact, it seemed something like a very very shortsighted creature wearing constantly stronger and better glasses, so that the eye looked daily farther and farther into the wonderful world ; daily widening the horizon, daily dispersing the film of ignorance, and seeing daily more clearly through the powerful lens of knowledge opportunities in the garden for beauties of form, colour, line and happiness. So ignorant I was ! I remember the day I went dreaming down a lane and stopped to lean on a low stone wall because the garden below flaunted a radiant troop of sapphire and violet " flags " ; the old woman leaned on her spade and watched me ; we talked of her pretty garden, and when I turned to go she offered me a root of the admired flag.

" 'Tain't the best time to move un, but this 'ull grow . . . ain't got no bloom on un, 'e ain't."

I thanked her, handling awkwardly and reverently the curious thick rhizome from which hung coarse fibres ; she saw inexperience in my manner.

" You'm from the hill up yonder, ain't you ? You'll need to gie un a bite o' loam ; 'tain't giving un a fair chanst to put un i' that thin sand o' yourn up there."

As she spoke another new world opened. A mother was created with her words ; the flower in my hand was weak, and alive, with needs ; I must not starve it—it depended on me for its chance in life : I learned in that dazzling instant that planting was a sacred responsibility. All the flowers I would ever plant in my garden for the rest of my life became my children.

" How do I get loam ? " I asked.

" Old Deadman 'e sells it," she answered, smiling at my eagerness, " 'e'll dror it in, three shillings a load 'e charges ; it's fair stuff ; eight or nine barrers to the load you gets. Shall I tell 'un you wants some ? "

Early next morning I was " barrowing loam," and since then it has been one of my liveliest occupations. I remember with what curiosity I examined it. . . What was loam like ? . . . Why was it loam ? . . . and why was my soil not loam ? . . . All these and a thousand questions bubbled in the brain while I hurried through dressing, having heard Old Deadman's cart busy in the lane soon after dawn. I sat on the barrow and handled his " loam." I had always thought that soil was soil and that flowers grew in it. That it had different characters had never occurred to me. What he had brought was dark stuff, a little sticky ; sticky enough to adhere if I squeezed a ball of it in my hand ; when I tried to do the same thing with my own garden soil it would not stick but ran through the fingers like sand through an hour glass. Also it was very pale and dry and easy to

dig in ; his felt heavier and had more " body."
As I worked I could feel somehow that there
was more substance, more nourishment, a
kinder diet in the imported than in the
indigenous soil ; and so I learned to know
sand from loam.

Old Deadman came up in the evening to
see if I could " do " with some more, and found
me hospitably enriching a long strip of ground
with the new loam. He watched approvingly
and then asked what was going in there.

" Hyssop," I said, in hot energy. " I want
to make herb borders to all these turf paths ;
rosemary for some, and sage, and lavender
for others."

" Doan't you go cloggin' of 'em up with this
'ere ; this is fit for roses, this is, and heavy
doers, like sweet peas. Rosemary, and them
there, like the sand, they do. They don't
want no loam."

I looked at the old man with ravenous
interest. Another flash to lighten my darkness. Then flowers and plants had individuality, temperament . . . it was not enough
to give them all loam. Some sickened with
rich fare, some pined without it. What

patience, what skill were needed to make a
happy garden !

I have never planted anything since then
without giving it, to the utmost of my ability,
the soil it likes to root in . . . and sometimes
it has meant a rare lot of asking and reading
to find what is wanted. In ordering from
nursery gardens, if the catalogue does not tell
me, I ask the firm ; and if a plant is given
I ask the giver, if he is the grower. It is
when a town friend sends me some prized
gem from a flower show that the puzzle sometimes comes in, because it never occurs to the
town dweller to put in a note saying " this
plant needs such an aspect and such a soil."
To him—as originally to me—" plants is
plants," and so I have to endure the buffetings
and inconveniences of that ignorance, of
which I am only just slowly learning to cease
to be an able exponent. It is more or less
tolerable to endure inconveniences one's self
for lack of knowledge (ignorance is really
laziness). There is a rough justice in it, and
justice is a glorious tonic, but always, always,
the young and helpless and innocent things
suffer for the ignorance of those they depend

on, animals, flowers, children. The possession of anything that depends on one's kindness is a tremendous responsibility. I tremble
to think of the light heart with which I have
entered into possession.

I remember the day I realised gardens were
really character sketches ; I was looking from
a train at the slipping landscape, idly loving
the moving trees, the running shadows ;
nearing Waterloo I noticed how the houses
were built closer together, how the gardens
grew niggardly, land more precious. We began
to pass a long row of small villas with narrow
strips of land lying towards the railway ;
there was the most astonishing difference in
the treatment of those uniform unpromising
slips of soil. A curious thought occurred to
me,—" I believe one's garden is *one's self.*"
I leaned forward looking eagerly—this man
loves colour, he is sensuous, artistic, ardent ;
from end to end of his narrow allowance
beautiful shades mingle and riot . . . this
man is very conventional, he is cramped
in his ideas ; he has the usual path, the usual
round bed, the usual everything which makes
the usual bore—this man has a slattern for

a wife, the washing is hung out and there is no garden, only a strip of moth-eaten turf; the washing shows no signs of children; perhaps they drink—they certainly do not love flowers—this man is a genius in design, he has laid out his plot to look three times as big as any one else's, he is a man of individuality—moreover, his influence is plain in the next four or five gardens lessening in intensity as they recede like circles in smitten water—here is a greedy man, he has tried to get everything, he even has a tiny greenhouse and kitchen garden—the train whirled by and I sat chewing the cud of this new idea.

I recalled gardens nearer home;—there was the jolly sportsman at Ardene, whom I knew for a good gambler and an industrious bridge player; it was quite in keeping with his character that he should make exhibition growing his hobby in the garden. Why, of course he would, a man like that! He would love the fight, the exhilaration of uncertainty, the tonic of a rattling good win. A straight enemy, a generous enemy, a smiling loser,—I knew him for all those and remembered with a sigh of perfect envy his wonderful sweet peas. The Master and I go to see them sometimes shod in humility; over a hill and down a dale followed by two sheep dogs, and so to a creeper-covered house where the winning flowers grow, the envy of all other amateurs, and their despair. Single stems of unimagined thickness tower aloft (he has to pick his sweet peas with a ladder); linen is stretched over some of the delicate shades to guard their colour from too much rain or sun; stalks there are bearing seven blooms; we look at the huge waxy petals, the enormous leaves like cabbages, marvel anew at the powerful fragrance, bow for the thousandth time to the toil such excellence has meant.

I wonder if anything will ever make an exhibition grower of me. I begin to think it is a special breed and that I do not belong to it. Exhibition growing means the merciless sacrifice of innumerable blooms, to ensure the surpassing excellence of one or two. Now, although I am heart and soul with the Eugenic Society, and talk dogmatically in season and out of season, and on the least provocation, about the principles there involved, I cannot carry my theories into practice when I get into the rose garden. It appals, it makes me go cold as I walk round the beloved beds, each unit in each of which is an intimate friend, to picture the inhuman excellence of óne or two solitary blooms on each tree if I were to sacrifice the whole glowing perfumed mass of roses waiting in the fold of bud to break into the sunshine. I have set forth more than once to show roses, and recoiled invariably before the task of sacrificing the lovely though possibly imperfect potential blooms. After all, one pleases one's self with one's garden, and if I like my beds brimful of scent and colour, the exhibition blooms are my loss and no óne else's.

Other types of gardens and gardeners floated into my brain as I pursued this strange thought that gardens are an open transcript of one's self for all the world to see; I remembered one set forth in square blocks of uncompromising colour, devoid of tenderness, inspiration or imagination, where a woman toils worthily laying out her staring colours and dogmatic lines. A sort of terror gripped me as I considered how merciless was the index it gave to a hard woman of strong political leanings, inelastic, barren, bitter.

I revolved other types : five acres in Cornwall devoted to varieties ; one tract given over to, say, tritomas, another to lilies, another to croci, another to irises, and so on, each tract containing every known variety of its kind ; the garden of a student, a scientist, almost monastic in its severe intellectuality ; a signpost, I realised, to the personality of the brilliant author of " Carnival." My own garden gave me pause ; I reviewed it with severe heartsinking, and realised it is not one garden at all but a collection of gardens ! An eruption of little successes, punctuated with vivid failures ; tortuous, Machiavellian, picturesque ; a tentative garden, where colour and design struggle for expression at the hands of a novice.

I began to feel that more than anything in the world a garden betrays personality ; it is a pitiless record, as accurate as the wave length of the red line in cadmium ; so plainly writ for the observant eye that there is almost a feeling of invading privacy in coming in

contact with a fresh one; the bias of its
owner's mind is indicated, the range of his
ideals, his perseverance or slackness in reaching
to them, his love of order, or disorder, his
education, his breed, his nature, are laid bare
to every eye; his very essence discovered.
I remembered with exquisite pleasure Mr.
Geoffrey Hurd-Wood's garden at Whitmead
Hill; a tiny place, so justly designed as to
give that idea of size and space which can
only be achieved with perfect proportion.
He designed and laid out the garden himself,
and it bears in every line the impress of a
cultured man at work on a congenial task.
A glade, a fountain, a tree—what are they
in most gardens? Accidents muffled in
excuse, if not ostentatious intrusions. Here
in the hands of a sympathetic artist they
are eloquent instruments of beauty. Stone
is used lavishly but with method; colour
is there rippling and flowing in admired
disorder; a far vista across Surrey is the whole
seeming reason for the design, and so harmonious is it that the garden seems to lead
to the country and each belong to each.
Wide shallow stone steps make way to a

A GLIMPSE OF MR. GEOFFREY HURD-WOOD'S BEAUTIFUL GARDEN

fountain in the centre. The entire idea is one of suggestion, too delicate to be described, too successful for analysis ; a rounded gem hidden away in the pines on a Surrey hill.

I make no pretentions to anything as coherently lovely in this my garden of ignorance. It is only three acres of rough pine wood and sandy scrub which in four years, through sloughs of direst mistake, have evolved into a rose garden, a terrace set with herbaceous beds, a tiny rock garden, herb garden, croquet lawn, orchard, asparagus beds, and kitchen garden. No one could start with less knowledge than I, and I am very sure that what I have achieved any other body may.

The longer I live the more do I grow to believe I am just like everyone else ; I mean that I am bored by what bores them, and cheered by what cheers them, and so on. A severe upbringing ground into the very fibres of me a belief that I was, beyond the average, stupid and unbelievably ignorant, so that for many years I hesitated to ask for information, and certainly did not dare to criticise the methods of those who gave it. Now that

I am declining on middle age I begin to perceive that I am not really so very stupid, and with this pleasing idea is born the courage to say what I think. And I think most garden books are dull. Frightfully dull. I could mention one or two, only decency forbids ; they lay down the law, and anyone who does that is a bore. They seem upside down, they tell one eternally to do this and to do that, without ever waiting to take breath and let the novice know what he is doing it all for, what lovely reward awaits his labour ! It is always " Now is the time to—" and " Now is the time to—" never " Now is the bloom time of so and so, and thus and thus do they look ! " So I am going to write of gardening as I would have liked to read of it ; while those who disapprove of my way have the comfort of knowing that mine is the only one of its kind, and the others of theirs are legion.* This book will be very little technical, because I know still so little it were folly to compete with others

* I would like here to offer my thanks to the Editor of *The Lady* (in which paper I wrote gardening articles for many months), for permission to use much of that work in this book.

who know all. (The letters F.R.H.S. look very grand, but they do not mean I have done anything to deserve them. Anyone can have them who cares to become a Fellow and partake of the advantages of the Royal Horticultural Society.)

One or two kind critics have told me that cats and pigeons and dogs and bees and photography are irrelevant, indeed unbecoming, to a garden book ; but there I wholly disagree. This book is only for people who, having found themselves in possession of a garden, may like to know some of the various ways in which happiness can be had out of it. I believe many people living in London smother a deep love of and desire for the companionship of a cat or dog or both, because of conscience, a kindly conscience, which tells them truly enough that animals are at their best and happiest when they have a garden to play in. The animal that loves one is really a very wonderful thing with its ridiculous pathetic faith, its desperate trust in our good will. I know, none better, that neither the bobtails nor the blue Persians are the best gardeners in the world, but the damage they do is really little in proportion to their companionship, which is much. It would be a lonely excursion to set forth on a day's bulb planting if I were not preceded to the scene of action by a sheep-dog ambling like a great bear, and followed by a snuffling Pekingese and two or three cats. They play all the time, generally knocking over the bulb bags, and mixing up the " special varieties " ; Bouncer always has his nose in the bone meal sack ; the little Pekingese follows the trowel, busily rooting out the freshly planted bulbs, so there is not a moment's dullness for anyone ; then a good many smacks go round, till lunch or tea is announced, and off the procession starts to the house, full of mutual esteem. I think birds and animals are *part* of a garden book.

Gardening seems like no other art—it engenders the kindest fellow-feeling everywhere ; indeed the countryside is an open book for the ignorant beginner ; every cottager will give his hint for the best upbringing of this and that, every gardener lends a willing ear to a knotty problem ; the special knowledge gathered through years of labour breast to breast with mother earth flower-lovers willingly spill for every questioner. There is nothing mean in them, nothing but immense comradeship and fellow feeling, so that the learner is armoured from the start if he will take trouble to ask questions fearlessly. The scores of clever technical books which are to be had for the buying leave no excuse for mistakes if he devours all !

Strange virtues one learns in a garden— virtues that have no place in London life, that would indeed be a nuisance there. First, foremost, deepest, one learns patience, humility in the constant service of a greater than one's self ; unselfishness, gratitude ; strange useless qualities accumulating unconsciously in those minds which offer a willing service to Nature, like the soft grey lichen on weathered stonework. I look back with gladness to the day when I found the path to the land of heart's desire, and thank Fate ceaselessly with a loud voice that she did not permit town to sap all the years away while the heart was turning to wind-voices and flower-faces and the hands of kindly earth.

CHAPTER II

BORDERS

WHEN I said to the Nursery Garden foreman, "What do you do?" I meant, "What sort of rose is your special province?" because I believed, in the perfection of my ignorance, that the only flowers which really needed expert culture were roses, and that the rest of a gardener's time went to the kitchen produce. His answer, "I do the 'erbaceous borders, mem," conveyed no more to me than that I had overlooked herbs in the programme of a nursery gardener's work, and that possibly mint and sage and all the rest of it *might* need a special man to grow them. It was long before I rightly understood what a herbaceous border meant, and that it need have no relation whatever to herbs proper. The whole idea of a herbaceous border came instinctively

when I set apart a wide space to take the
" muddle " (everything was a " muddle "
when I wanted some of it and had not space
to make a special garden of it, like a pæony
garden or iris garden) ; snapdragons, Canterbury bells, pinks, phloxes, sweet williams,
all the other indispensables were put, without
method, into this large space till the illuminating day when someone said, " You have quite
a good herbaceous border coming along here "
—and a fact was added to the diary :—

" The muddle bed is a herbaceous border."

In the core of my heart, where technical
terms are disliked, it has always remained
the muddle bed.

The great blue delphiniums have become
very popular of recent years ; every cottage
has its brilliant clump, and in the stately
borders of large country houses they play a
highly important part. As far as names of
varieties go, I am a broken reed to lean on ;
but though I do not know their catalogued
names, there is a pleasing collection in full
bloom at this moment. I ordered " a dozen
strong clumps of delphinium " in the early
days of my gardening, and the order evidently

fell into conscientious hands, for here is a fine range of shades, and I do not want to know what they are called or to get any more. I let a spike or two go to seed every year, and when they are ripe I go round some dry, warm evening to collect the shiny black seeds. Formerly I would go with a lot of little boxes (generally nougat ones, the three-penny size), and these were duly labelled something after this fashion :—" The pale blue next the Canterbury bells," " The dark purple behind the red-hot poker," " The bright blue next the biggest Tausendschön," and so on. These boxes were numbered, and when the seeds were sown in separate patches they were numbered to correspond, and the seedlings were planted out cunningly to make clumps to shade. But the bees or winds made mock of me. The delphiniums come up just as they like, in shades of their own choosing, very lovely, and very various. So now they are collected indiscriminately, and strong young plants are planted out from time to time to take the place of any clumps which are showing signs of age. The more beautiful colours can always be perpetuated by cuttings

or root division. Delphiniums like a deep
cool soil, but can be grown with culture on
hot, dry sand, as my borders prove to all
who care to look. In planting, dig deep
on either clay or sand. Clay wants to be
lightened and made friable; sand wants
strengthening with rich farmyard manure.
In hot summers a good drenching with liquid
manure from time to time is a great help,
and I always see to it that a mulch goes over
the plants in spring. It is one of the joys of
spring gardening to watch the thick, fleshy
stems of the delphiniums pushing strongly
up to the light; they are handsome things,
often the reddish colour of tea rose foliage,
and break into feathery graceful leaf; gardeners on heavy soil might remember that
these flowers need perfect drainage. If one
does not mind waiting, and is content to
leave colour to fate, it is undoubtedly cheapest
to raise these flowers from seed. Sown in
late spring they will bloom a little next year,
and in the following summer have grown into
strong crowns. In that way an outlay of a
shilling or so will stock a large border. Fine
plants to name may be bought at anything

from 9d. to 3s. 6d. a plant, and these, planted in autumn, will yield great spikes of colour next season. To protect the crowns from slugs in spring and winter it is a wise plan to strew coal ashes over them. True Blue is an intense deep blue, Beauty and Belladonna fine pale blues, I have learned on good authority. Mixed colours cost about 5s. 6d. a dozen plants, or two guineas a hundred.

Whenever I dream of an English cottage garden, I see a little lane of Madonna lilies leading to the humble door, and many an exquisite moment of dreams-come-true has been mine when I have found the cottage and the lane ! They are by no means uncommon. Our British workman has in him a beautiful love of gardens. So by millstream, by roadside, by hayfield, you will find the thatched, half-timbered cottage, and leading to its creeper-clad portal an avenue of Madonna lilies, often backed by hollyhocks, edged with lavender. And how they grow, those stately lilies with their golden throats ! They seem to thrive anywhere, though I know they hate a stagnant soil. In the summer dusk, exhaling their powerful sweetness, they would make a poet of the veriest clod. In my garden they grow among a pink-flowered plant, called I believe, rose campion. It seeds freely, has a silvery foliage with the texture of plush, and grows among the lilies with a high free-branching habit ; the colour of the flower is a bright rosy magenta, which sounds ugly enough, but is in reality a brilliant foil to the satin-white of the lilies. They make great demands on patience, the prime virtue of a gardener, these Madonna lilies : they want wonderful patience, for they establish themselves so slowly, and hate to be disturbed. They start into growth very early, and must be planted among the first of autumn bulbs. It is wise to order them in late summer, and to see that in planting they have a well-drained site, are not near fresh manure, and are set in a little sharp sand. It is recommended by some gardeners to dust the bulbs with dry flower of sulphur before planting, to help in keeping away disease.

I have just been round looking at everything in the garden, for this is the time of the year that I would like to push back with both hands, that it may not come and pass so quickly. Every hour has its unfolding flower, every path its lovely nook new set in bloom. The daffodils have raced away, the cottage tulips are hurrying through their prime. Cherry tree and pear have snowed their petals, apple trees are flushing warm through the valley, and here are the lilacs breaking their bowls of spikenard to all the airs of heaven. More and more as the garden grows dearer one learns to wonder at any choosing to live in town, and to grieve for those living there who would fain be in the country. The latter is the tragedy. The first man does not know what he misses, has no need of it, suffers no pain or loss ; but the other—I had it very badly, a desire so fierce, so lasting, that all the rest of life given to a garden and the country will not obliterate or wholly assuage the memory of it.

In the wood foxgloves are throwing up sturdy shoots. They love shade, and revel among the heather, gorse, and bracken. The white and yellow brooms are coming out ; lovely though the yellow are, they cannot compare with the bridal beauty of the white.

There are some great bushes near a hedge of arbor vitæ at the end of the rose garden ; they shine purely against that dark insistent background. Brooms are tiresome things to prune ; they may be cut back in the young stuff (which, by the way, spoils their long switch effect), but one must not cut the old wood on any account ; well-rooted plants hate to be disturbed, though young pot plants transplant readily ; they like light soil.

It is hard to remember, looking round the garden now, how bare it was in winter, and how bravely the eye of faith saw the colour to be. I walk among the beds and picture again the bare earth, the sticks and labels ; the tufts of hardy occasional green which were the garden so little while ago ; and then I look at the white and blue and gold, the crimson and purple, the grey and green which are the garden now, and gratitude, joy, and wonder bubble within me for the thousandth time. There is no happiness so tender and so invigorating as this happiness of tending flowers, except that lovelier one of tending babies and young animals.

D

Which reminds me that I have made a painful discovery—cats like to roll in nemophila. I sowed a wide border of this pretty annual in the autumn, and instead of the close carpet of starry blue which should be now glorifying a long herbaceous bed, there are a few jagged patches struggling for life. As the quaint white-spotted leaves pushed through the ground the big father-cat discovered them and rolled on them. One could almost imagine he knew how fine his long blue-grey fur looked against that azure background, and how his orange eyes flashed out like flame ! I talked to him a good deal and sent him away ; but he came back every time, and at last his wives found him there and rolled too. I think I shall sow a border next year near their house in the kitchen garden, and let them have it all to themselves. I don't like sharing it.

The perfumes of spring ! Under the shady north-east wall the lilies-of-the-valley are thick and waxen-white, and in the pine wood are three good patches, healthy and happy, open to the early morning sun. Two of those same are in full bloom but one is only leaf.

I was decoyed by a pleasing advertisement in a gardening paper which offered two hundred and fifty " strong flowering crowns " for 5s. It is the worst policy to buy cheap garden stuff. Labour and time (most valuable of a gardener's allies) are wasted. It is much better to buy less and buy that good. I have proved it over and over again, and every time I pass those flaunting lily leaves, all barren of flowers, I remember that the same postal order would have brought me a hundred fine crowns, a joy to look upon now, if I had been less greedy. The border under the kitchen window is the one which pleases me most sincerely this year. I knew the plants were too crowded and the soil worn, so the second week in October I forked them out very carefully. They made a strange sight on the grass, matted together in a solid mass, crying bitterly for more room. They were laid aside carefully, " heeled in," while I dug out the old soil all along the border two feet deep and more. The bottom of the trench I then layered with the usual friend, well-rotted manure, and over that was sifted fine loam, with which I mixed some bone-meal. Then the strongest crowns were put back (each with three or four inches of root) about six inches apart, and left to establish themselves.

The violets are over now but they flourished merrily in many a shady corner ; somehow they have become associated in my mind with craft and theft, because they represent various barrow-loads of loamy clay stolen from the roses. In this garden—perched on the side of a pine and heather hill—some special flowers (roses and pæonies) are afforded the expensive luxury of made-up beds, and I am so cursed with the gardener-conscience that every time I wheel a barrow load of rich cool soil away from the rose garden I feel that pale Annie Müller, and sturdy Sunburst, and delicate Lady Hillingdon, and all the rest of them, are standing on tip-toe watching me in an incredulous amazed alarm. It is really a silly trick to take any of it—they need every spoonful, dear, greedy things—but the violets are very grateful. The best position for them is under a north hedge or on a north or north-west shrubbery border, where they can have partial shade with a free current of air. They like rich loamy soil. I grow La France and Princess of Wales; they increase freely and are easy to propagate.

Under the lilacs, the guelder rose, and all the hedges are the starry primroses; there are only a few straggling blooms left now, but they have been very good; they never fail. Year after year they beam through the grass, and regularly year by year do I bless them with a fresh impulse of gratitude; for primroses love cool clay, and this soil is poor fare for them indeed. They look indescribably fair among the oak and brass and copper of the cottage when gathered and arranged, with their leaves among them, in a big shallow brass bowl.

A finely polished Spanish brassero, or an old refectory bowl, filled flush with newly plucked primroses, set in a dim corner of a cottage room on the glossy surface of an oaken gate-legged table, gives an effect of pure flame, a spot of glowing pallor, which does no other flower that I know of; the perfume of primroses is one of the sweetest, freshest things in the world. They like a cool soil and shady situation, but will grow almost anywhere, and can be moved practically at any time. The real way to stock one's garden with primroses is not to buy them in cold blood at all but to go to some neighbouring copse or wood with trowel and trug, and *steal* them. There is a flavour about them ever after which no other flower in your garden can give you. At least, one supposes not. In good soil it is well worth while growing the beautiful bunch primroses, creamy white and deep rich gold ; but it was not till I went over to see them blooming in the nurseries one spring that I personally knew how fine these flowers were, because they grow sulkily, even pathetically, on my soil.

Obviously lilacs are slow growers ! When they arrive at a certain stature they seem to be sure bloomers ; but they take time to get there and are chary of their favours in youth. It is with considerable excitement that I find a lot of bloom on the two special lilacs which have been sulking for three years at the far end of the terrace behind the heleniums. When I saw them first they were blooming beautifully in pots, a deep double purple one and a very handsome double white. They were 5s. 6d. each, which made them an extravagance, of course ; but the nurseryman assured me so heartily that they were healthy, and would soon make " grand bushes " that they were carried home and planted with a good dressing of short manure. For two or more years they did not add an inch to their stature ; they remained alive and that was all. I was in despair, and asked everyone what the reason might be. No one seemed to know anything about them until an extremely civilised and very smart lady, who had come down for the day in a Paris gown and high-heeled shoes and a closed car, walked round the garden with me after lunch. She held her gown well up, away from thorny rose-sprays and purple pæony pollen and all the other perils that beset nice clothes in a garden. She was very bored, and so, I fear, was I. When we were passing the two little disgraces I pointed them out perfunctorily, and said they were obstinate and hard to please. She said, " Have you tried them with plenty of lime yet ? " I said " No," and spent the rest of the time she was with me in wondering how much more she knew; if, indeed, she knew that, or if she made it up to fit the environment of her day ; if she had been countrybred, and this was a sudden beam of remembered lore ; if she had read it in some novel ; in fact, that question of hers interested me more than anything she had said, or looked, or been, ever since I had known her, which was long and superficially. It was the one only symptom of garden intelligence she ever betrayed. I distrusted it so much that I hesitated long before I would try it. But last autumn in despair I put a thick dressing of lime round them, and chanced the wisdom of my guest. It is very interesting to find them now smothered in bloom ! I hand on the information for what it may be worth.

The yellow border looks very jolly and promising ; it starts early in the year with a border of golden pansies. Mrs. S. A. Cade is the variety—a pansy with a strong sweet scent like honey, that starts flowering in February. These are followed by a thick clump of creamy yellow flags ; then Spanish irises, yellow and Thunderbolt bronze. There is a little group of Austrian Copper briar roses at the far end, a big sulphur-coloured tree lupin, half a dozen strong brown and yellow heleniums, and some carefully chosen cactus dahlias, varying from pale yellow to brilliant flame. A good flower to put in a bronze or yellow bed is montbretia. There is a border of them along a kitchen garden path ; there they bloom in autumn like a form of iris. When it is difficult to spare precious blooms for the house from the terrace beds I can go to this border and pluck regardless. Vases full of brilliant flame-colour look well against the cream distempered walls.

Montbretias are curious things to deal with. They want a rich light soil, and then they increase at a terrific speed. Every two or three years (some gardeners say every year) they have to be lifted, and good single bulbs separated from the mass of roots and bulbs, which have multiplied where originally one was planted. If they are left unseparated they do not bloom.

Taking it all in all they led me a merry dance. I found the first few bulbs in the garden in the days when every flower was a stranger and a miracle to me. Being seized with intense admiration for their sturdy manner, lovely deep orange colour and iris-like form, I made the usual pilgrimage to neighbouring cottages (I had not then got a gardener) to find what these precious flowers were. Having learned they were montbretias I ordered some more to increase my stock, and then discovered that this extravagance was totally unnecessary, inasmuch as they increased the following year with an extra-ordinary rapidity. Being a sincere admirer of their beauty, I was quite able to put up with the quantity, and rejoiced with no mean spirit the following summer to find a perfect forest of the orange blooms. The gardener agreed with me in admiring them very much, and then told me it would be as well in the autumn to separate the bulbs, selecting only the strongest, replanting them singly, and giving away the surplus. I was astonished when I set to work on the job to discover what an enormous increase there was. We laid out a fine bed, and there followed the summer of 1911 with its protracted drought, which effectually killed the lot. I think I have now about half a dozen survivors. They seem to have no sense of proportion. They must be all or nothing, like people in love.

AFTER LONG DELIBERATION A CLEARANCE WAS DECIDED UPON

THE EFFECT

The great narcissus family is over now.
It is good to see the golden bells fluttering
over grass in the April weather, and so I have
them on slopes in corners, among foxgloves
in the wood, in shady dells, and along far-off
borders, thickly set in successional varieties
to dance their little hour in the ballroom of
the spring. Personally I never appreciated
the daffodil until I came to have a garden.
It conveyed to me only an impression of tight
yellow bunches disgorged by Covent Garden
on to the London streets, yellow bunches
that had no perfume, and rustled like paper
flowers or dry wheat-ears when handled. I
wonder if other people notice that sound of
daffodils ? When one holds a bunch, the
thick green stems squeak a little, and the
yellow heads rustle like thin paper. That
is how these April flowers became woven into
the fibre of my memory. Always the scentless yellow cups borne nodding and rustling
down dust-blown London streets to the tune
of " Fourpence a bunch," " Threepence a
bunch," bought by housewives for the cheap-
ness of them and the love of the spring they
meant, and taken away in hot gloved hands

with paper round their noisy stalks. Then one day I saw them blowing in the garden of the " Spotted Cow " the little inn in the valley. They grew in large clumps under every tree, in every border, great golden patches of double yellow, nodding and dancing in the wind. They looked so fair, so fittingly set against the dark, sweet-smelling soil, that the heart ached for joy at meeting them and for pity of their brethren in the City streets. They became from that moment new flowers in my mind : wild, shy, free things that one always wanted to see growing, and never, never picked. And now, after many days, I have them blowing in the wood and on the lawns, under hedges and trees, in a long succession of varieties. I do not put many of them in the terrace borders, because I find the bulbs get so cut up and disturbed in the autumn, when spade and fork are busy there; and I also labour under a conviction that they do not like the stable manure to which the herbaceous stuff is treated in the fall of the year. Moreover, all daffodils prefer partial shade to the clear open, so I see they get it, and very bravely they respond. In the woods are sheets of yellow trumpets and fragrant white pheasant's-eye narcissus ; under the apple tree by the sundial a cunning choice of varieties has made yellow trumpets bloom from early March to May ; and the beloved old-fashioned " double daffs " star the green and brown of every hedge with brilliant constellations.

I always plant as early as possible in the autumn, as early as I can get orders supplied, and the fascination of experimenting with new varieties is tremendous. There are over two thousand named sorts, ranging in price from 9d. per dozen to £50 a bulb. It is possible to plant as late as Christmas, but the blooms are so much taller and stronger if put in early that I would sooner go without than do them the injustice of planting late. For preference they should have a deep, rather moist, loam. If it has been freshly dug before planting, the soil should be left for a fortnight or so to settle before the bulbs are put in ; and if at digging seven or eight ounces of basic slag is dressed to the square yard, the preparation for planting may be considered good. My own soil being, as I have said, of the lightest, driest, and sandiest, I prefer to work in crushed bones (about an ounce and a half to the square yard), and then, after planting, to sprinkle about three-quarters of an ounce of sulphate of potash to the square yard over the surface. Potash has the blessed virtue of retaining moisture in the soil (a condition which daffodils seem to demand imperatively); experts declare it also increases the depth of colour in the flowers, but it must be used sparingly, not at the rate of bones or slag. Although they like shade and a cool soil, it is unwise to plant under heavy drip from branches, or where the main roots of the trees come close to the surface. They should be planted not too deep, and not too shallow. A good rule advocated by the most famous growers is to cover the bulbs with soil once and a half their own depth (measuring the bulb from the collar of its neck to its actual base). On good ordinary loam they should be left undisturbed for years, but on my light sand they have to be lifted and helped oftener than this lazy soul approves.

A deplorable spectacle, to my way of thinking, is presented by daffodils growing in rows or circles. The way to do is to take the bulbs and throw them where they are to grow, and plant them where they fall. They look thin and straggly if set too far apart, and yet some few stragglers at the edges of a bold group add greatly to the grace of grouping. Used with sympathetic intelligence, they are the most decorative of flowers; used stupidly, they are indescribably boresome.

Canterbury bells and snapdragons are coming along, London pride will soon be making a proud and feathery display in the cottage gardens. The tree pæonies are budding freely. Along the back border heavy-budded pinks are stirring the warm air with promise of fragrance to be. I am glad now that I spent the whole of a long day in early spring with those same pinks. There was a barrowload of loam lying temptingly disengaged just inside the wood, so I set forth with spade and sieve and sifted as much again of fine leaf mould and light sandy garden soil into it. Then I got half a dozen good heaped trugs of short well-rotted manure, and mixed the whole together into a rich compost. The rest of the day was spent in digging cautiously

among pink plants, and removing by trowel-
fuls at a time the old worn-out soil, then
working the new rich mixture carefully and
thoroughly among the roots. The young
fibres appear to have quickly discovered the
refreshing fare, and the grey-green foliage
of the plants, which is as lovely in its pale
sobriety as the flowers themselves, lies thick
and close along the edge of the turf path which
it flanks.

The muddle beds are really as interesting
as any in the garden, though I feel I am only
at the beginning of learning how to manage
them, slowly groping to the idea that simplicity of grouping is the thing to aim at
rather than diversity of subjects; and to my
mind simplicity of grouping does not necessarily mean violence of contrast.

I remember happening on the following in
Mr. Rogers' charming book, " Garden Planning "—" Were I planting a bed of two
contrasting colours I should adopt the simple
plan of using a broad edging of one colour,
with a central mass of the other. A bed of
white pinks edged with mauve violas, or
purple blue Canterbury bells edged with

yellow violas, or with the yellowish green foliage of the pyrethrum would entirely satisfy my sense of a good colour effect," and I remember how I quarrelled with him in my mind for a whole long summer afternoon over that paragraph.

I never met Mr. Rogers, nor do I know him in any way, but we had a long and violent wrangle all the same. As fast as I set my disagreement with him, the obstinate little just bit of my mind, which never gives me any peace, would bob up and tell me *his* side of the question. I could not digest those last few words : "would entirely satisfy my sense of a good colour effect."

To be entirely satisfied with a bed of white pinks edged with mauve violas, or a bed of purple blue Canterbury bells with yellow violas, or indeed with the yellowish green foliage of the pyrethrum, makes me feel as I used to feel as a child when my bedroom wall was covered with texts and the horizon of Sundays was bound with the Collect I had to learn ; I mean the hard-and-fastness of it all filled me as those childish things filled me, with a very fury of revolt. I do not think

E

a bed of anything has ever satisfied my sense
of a good colour effect. Nothing less than
the whole sky and the landscape within it,
and the light of the sun, and the beauty
of the seasons can satisfy my greed for colour
and brim each nerve to overflowing with the
elixir of beauty; so that I really believe it
is harmony and proportion that I worship
in the muddle beds more than the brilliant,
persistent spots of colour.

A very large proportion of nearly every
garden book is devoted to the scientific dis-
cussion of the construction of herbaceous
borders, and those who run may read. The
muddle bed is really the land of happy ex-
periments, and the enthusiast's school-room.
It is from season to season that one notices
how well the bloom time of such a plant and
the colour and the habit of it accord with
the same in such another, and into the garden
diary goes a note to plant these two in
sufficient quantities next year in juxta-
position.

It is easy enough for one to make a list of
herbaceous plants which accord well together,
and are the usual inhabitants of herbaceous

borders ; but in that way dogma creeps in, the hateful fetters of " thus and thus shalt thou do," and the complete stifling of individuality. I am too happy wrestling with the problems of my muddle beds to attempt to dictate to my fellows. As the years go I shall learn what colours please best, and what sequence gives the kindest range of time, and plant accordingly, but not for worlds would I follow anyone else's scheme ! The whole essence of joy, if one loves the garden, is to struggle to the ideal beauty in one's own pig-headed way.

CHAPTER III

COLOUR SCHEMES

THE only way to wrestle out colour-schemes in a garden is to keep a garden diary and note in it what blooms with what, and when ; then if one is very enthusiastic one can go on to describe at length what effect each combination makes.

Out of my ignorance I have learned that. It is one of the things I would really offer as advice to the happy beginner. Keep a garden diary. Note week by week what is blooming, and compare year by year the differences in dates. It is astonishing to learn how elastic bloom time is. I hate advice, it is nearly always an impertinence, but I have a few morsels to offer, for all that. Keep a garden diary, and let your garden be your own expression of what you love in gardens. Don't let every comer sway you to his way and to hers. Have your *own* garden ! I know all this has been thought of before and done before by White in " Selborne," but I did not know it till I had dredged the notion for myself out of the waters of ignorance and failure. And anyway it does not hurt to repeat it, because it may come to some readers still as a new idea. It is a very sound one, it involves trouble, but then everything that is worth doing does that.

Personally I set colour before most things, before exhibition blooms, before new varieties, before (to my shame) design, and I have found that the garden I want, a garden of perfectly satisfying colour, will take seven times seven years and more to make ! I work so slowly. The iris garden is an example ; I have made it now beyond the rose garden in front of the wood. It would be difficult to exaggerate the value of those cool clear blues between the hot scarlets and pinks of the rose-beds and the sombre evergreen of the pine wood. But the idea did not come all at once ; it evolved through two summers from long broody evenings when the eye dwelt (for all its pleasure

something still discontent) on the roses blooming up to the very brim of the wood. I
learned it was blue I wanted next to the wood
one evening when somebody came along with
a great armful of delphiniums ; but at first,
being lazy, I thought it would do to edge the
paths with Souvenir violas, a lovely searching
blue.

Ultimately I admitted that that would
not be bold enough, and autumn brought a
terrific upheaval in the existing scheme. The
roses were removed and rearranged, a little
lawn was laid down in the space so left, and
that in turn cut into beds and planted cunningly
with successive varieties of irises.

What extraordinary pleasure those flowers
give—Alata blooming gloriously from the last
week in October, followed by Reticulata in February and Sindjarensis in March—the pretty
blue and white iris from Mesopotamia ; Stylosa
(or, as accurate minds call it, Unguicularis)
carries its flowers of exquisite blue mauve,
twice as big as the biggest crocus, through
March to mid April and then the recitative
is bravely launched into May by the dwarf
bearded Crimean irises, to be followed by the

intermediate flags, and so on to the great
summer chorus of bulbous Spanish and English with their magnificent range of colour
and courage of growth.

Those little dwarf bearded fellows are very
nice in habit ; they only grow six to eighteen
inches high but have strong rhizomes like
the full-fledged flags their cousins, the same
wide spear-like leaves, and the selfsame
pleasing trick of increasing rapidly, a
tendency which commends them greatly to
the pocket. Pumila Coerulea the sky blue is
a good variety, so is Count Andrassy the
dark-veined azure, and another favourite is
Socrates the claret, with his yellow beard.

I have discovered a very charming colour
combination for a border to bloom in July
and August ; it is under a wall that is hung
with Virginian creeper—to the mad festivity
of earwigs. After the last late tulip has sped
its way and the last blood-red bloom is worn
upon the wallflowers, the border gets cleaned
out and given a " refresher " of loam ; in
front of the Virginian creeper go sturdy
seedling plants of white tobacco plant, in
front of these again a thick border of blue

double lobelia ; late in every summer the white lily flowers of the tobacco plants are in stately bloom, and the Virginian creeper is turning red and gold and brown (like the maple trees in Canada) when lobelia comes to its full glory.

The searching blue, compact and dwarf-growing, stretches its keen line in fine contrast to the waxen beauty of the tobacco-flowers, and they, in turn, stand gloriously against the fiery brilliance of Virginian creeper ; in the cool of the evening tobacco plants give their perfume and raise their white faces to the sky ; during the heat of the day they fold into a pathetic buff despair. From time to time I hold earnest debates with myself over that border. I want to plant it with azaleas, copper and gold and cream, for the spring, with strong bulbs of lilium auratum under their shade to make stately parade in August. But every planting time goes by and finds the border dedicated to wallflowers and tulips in spring, and the lobelia-tobacco lines in summer. So does sentiment wring us, making memories into habits.

There are some unexpected untried-for garden successes which give a great deal of pleasure ; those one has laboured for have dwelled so long in the imagination that when they effloresce into being there is rather the feeling of welcoming an expected friend than the thrill of suddenly encountering a new one. I shall not readily forget the delight I felt last May when I came up some steps in the wood upon an unexpected and lovely picture ; there, in a sunny patch, was a large plant of white broom, its feathery fairy sprays dancing like a veil of gossamer lace in the sunlight, and behind it in the shade a plant of the rhododendron Pink Pearl in full bloom. The blush of rose colour set in the sombre shade of pine trees was in itself very beautiful, but as I caught sight of it then, through a haze of glistening white broom, it made an unforgettable picture.

Talking of rhododendrons reminds me mine are growing apace; it seems slow to think that it will be another six or seven years before they make any great splash, but it is good to see the young shoots spreading and spreading every year. Most of the people I know

with gardens seem to have great bushes of them,
brilliant with colour ; my plants are all young
and still being mulched every year with farmyard manure to help them along. I shall
be glad when they are out of the nursery and
grown into sturdy bushes. They want to fill
out a good deal before they give the eye effect
they were planted for. I have them banked
at the end of the lawn under the dovecote, and
just on the edge of the pine wood. There they
get the necessary partial shade, and the perfect
background against which their great trusses
of colour can be fittingly set. Rhododendrons
grouped to colour make a magnificent decoration. Put in some significant spot in the
garden which gives the required aspect,
crimson inclining to scarlet, grouped with
dark claret colour and true pink, and you will
have a rich and glowing brocade for weeks.
It is not easy to do better than follow Miss
Jekyll's choice of varieties for such a scheme
as the above. Surely never was such a gardener as she is, so patient, so sincerely alive
to colour, so gentle in expression of opinion,
and every scheme she offers has been through
the mill of her personal experience.

The varieties she suggests for the red group are : Nigrescens, dark claret colour ; John Waterer and James Marshall Brook, both fine red crimsons ; Alexander Adie and Atrosanguineum, good crimson inclining to blood-colour ; Alarm, rosy-scarlet ; and Bianchi pure pink. This last is the only variety that Miss Jekyll will pass as a true pink without a suspicion of rank quality, though Kate Waterer and Sylph are both called by that colour, and are splendid varieties. Another colour group of great beauty is the cool purple and lilac-white combination. Any of the deep clear Ponticum class do for this effect, planted with Sappho, Album Elegans, a fine old free-growing kind, or Album Grandiflorum. Two other good lilac-whites are Luciferum and Reine Hortense. Rhododendron Ponticum is the old cool purple which grows wild in the woods, and is the commonest, though by no means the least beautiful of all. I think it must be often used as a stock to graft the newer varieties upon, else why the war upon the " suckers " which is advocated in March by experienced gardeners, and the strange combination of colour which may be seen occasionally upon the same plant ?

I always think of Sark, Swinburne's "Garden of Cymodoce," when the rhododendron trees are in bloom. The mental process is a complex one ; I think it is because of the pools in the rocks there, where the gorgeous florescent bosses of the sea-anemones make the tiny sea-gardens brilliant with colour, just as on a different scale do the bright bosses of rhododendron-flower in the garden.

In planting, there are a few important things to remember about these shrubs : they like partial shade, they abhor lime, and they revel in peat. In this poor soil here, I make a deep, very deep, and very wide hole, which is then filled with peat, leaf-mould, and loam. After planting the bush and treading it in firmly, a good top-dressing of farmyard manure goes round, and this labour is repeated with every rhododendron that is planted. It is slow and it is tiring, but the rewards are very great, and, to paraphrase the old saying, " quick planting makes slow growing."

One learns patience in a garden ; hurry seems vulgar after the stately deliberation of Nature has laid its broad palm across life ; the majestic rhythm of the seasons and the fertile calm of mother earth have a way of hushing the noisy heart like a divine rebuke—creation flourishes in silence, sterility in clamour . . . I believe that is not so clever as true. Anyhow, year by year the great pendulum swings from Christmas to Midsummer and in each tick gives the garden a few more inches of rhododendron, and do what I may I cannot hurry them, only help to a stronger stature with watching and feeding, and, in the first place, careful conscientious planting.

I have sometimes had a rare chase to get the exact colour I have admired in a flower, as, for example, this clump of pale blue pansies. I saw the colour first at Henley some summers ago, and it bit vividly into the memory. It was in the time of day when all the boats are packed so close that one can walk across the river on them, and a punt was next to ours with four people in it, two middle-aged, and two young. The young ones were so near to me that I could feel the tense electricity of the mute wooing that was in progress. Very fresh, grey-eyed, and Saxon they were to look upon. I trust that long before this they have settled the violent pleading of that hot afternoon. I know I, as a humble onlooker, wished them well enough. They both looked so nice. In the girl's white muslin dress were tucked a couple of dilapidated blue pansies. It was there I first saw the colour that I knew at once was the one colour I would like to mass in a garden ; an indescribable blue, clear and searching, with a hint of rosy lilac and a dark centre with a yellow eye, one of those simple cunning pansy faces that wins the heart. My enthusiasm for the garden has led me to many courageous acts, but it did not make me break into the drama in the next boat, so I did not ask the girl what the name of the variety was. I read descriptions in every catalogue, and looked out for it in flower shows ; but for long and long I could not find the beautiful colour. A description would read so like it that I would get a few plants to try, but always the colour was wrong—too harsh or too pale or too dark.

And only last year on a scented June evening, when I was dawdling home along a remote country lane, I saw the very pansy I wanted ; one plant in a little cottage garden. There was no one in, so I waited, and when the old man came home I asked him for the name of the pansy, or to be allowed to buy a cutting. He did not know the name, but said he would give me a cutting, or I could have the plant for a penny. That plant was so watched and tended that I almost feared it would die for spite ; but it made a dozen plants in due course. Fine young straight cuttings they were. Next May I shall have more than a hundred of them, and a splendid show they will make. A local nurseryman named the variety Souvenir when I showed him a bloom—a good enough name, seeing all the circumstances ! Pansies are best taken from cuttings if one wishes to ensure the correct colour. They are said to come true from seed. Perhaps I have been unlucky. I will not dogmatise, but they certainly do come true from cuttings. They look best massed in one variety, and make a magnificent carpet for beds of standard roses.

Two years ago I tried massing blood-red wallflowers and Thomas Moore tulips. A splendid fiery effect they gave too, but so many people have them nowadays that I have grown well weary of them, and am trying a more delicate scheme this year, with pale cream and deep gold wallflowers planted in a long border, with white tulips and just a few gold tulips among them. The variety of wallflowers are Cranford Beauty and Primrose Dame, which were raised from seed and pricked out into a nursery bed as soon as fit to leave the frame. The tulips mixed with them are L'Immaculae and Didieri Alba, two hundred of each, these being white varieties, and one hundred Bouton d'Or, to help the scheme of gold.

In one of the broad borders a space has been lavishly treated and planted with herbaceous pæonies, exquisitely fragrant varieties of cream singles, and flame-coloured semi-doubles ; in among them in the good soil are some very fine daffodil bulbs. It is an ideal combination, for neither of them ought to be disturbed for years, and the colour is good. The golden daffodil cups are framed in beauty by the red-brown foliage of the pæonies in their first growth, and later on the spreading leaves of the latter hide the dying spikes of the daffodils. It is perhaps as well to remark that pæonies do not give much show till they are established, and that they will probably need a year's grace. The plant will perhaps bloom the first season, but if it does not there need be no bitter disappointment. It will repay next year and every succeeding year with generous interest for the delay in starting, especially if it is planted in deep fertile soil, with some light protection from easterly winds. If I had room I would give up a whole border to these splendid plants, and have them in every variety, in every colour, and shape and scent.

I have one very promising plant in a corner of the lawn by the summer-house, where it is shaded from the early morning sun. For two years the whole family watched its slow and patient progress, till last May a swelling bud caused general excitement. I fancy few of us passed that plant, some time of the day or other, without giving it a canful of manure water " just to help it along " (everyone knowing full well that pæonies are gross

F

feeders and much beholden for any kind attentions at bloom time). When the green sheath began to burst, and pink showed through, we settled down to see what this much petted plant was going to do for us at last. It was about the same period that the Master bethought himself that the raven was tame enough to be pinioned and let loose, and we then discovered what a pestiferous pet a raven can be in a garden.

He really liked most of all to terrify the cats, but after these diversions his hobby was nipping off all the bright coloured flowers. He went for all the late tulips and early irises, and was then discovered by the horrified gardener making for the treasured pæony bloom. A grating, or prison house, of wire was therefore constructed over the pæony to protect it from the savage assault of the black devil we had let loose in the garden, and which nobody had the courage to catch. Under that hideous mask the great pink bud expanded, bloomed, and finally faded, so that now and for ever in my mind are indissolubly connected wire netting and tree pæonies.

A raven is a curious pet at the best of times ;
he is a carnivorous bird and likes to hide bits
of meat at the back of his house or in odd
corners ; when they are very smelly and
unpleasant he goes and eats them. Our
raven has developed a sentimental affection
for Bouncer, the sheep-dog. If anyone pets
the dog the raven gets behind him in jealous
despair and pulls his trousers hard, so that
the harassed animal is divided between the
pestilence at his heels and the pleasing attentions in front. When he goes off and lies in
the shade by himself the raven hops after him
with the queer one-sided gait his cropped wing
gives him, and stands as near to Bouncer's
nose as he can possibly get, ruffling up all
his feathers and looking ineffably foolish and
sentimental. It is difficult to imagine anything more ridiculous than the doting glances
that disagreeable bird casts upon this sole
object of his adoration. He does not care
for any of the other dogs, in fact we always
suspect him of wanting to make a meal off
the Pekingese's bulgy eyes ; indeed, one can
well imagine that they might be irritating
and suggestive to a bird of prey, they are so

impudently bright and prominent and tempting. The raven not only imitates the sheepdog's bark so faithfully that we can hardly tell which of them it is, but he has taught himself to whistle for him and to call him by name in a rasping husky voice, which, until he got used to it, seemed to cause Bouncer a good deal of soul searching; I think he thought it was the gardener in a temper.

He is terrible as an army with banners to many of our guests. It is not an uncommon sight at the week-end to find nobody stirring out of the front door without a stick. I well remember the anæmic young nursemaid who brought a friend's baby down from town. She was a very languid young person and looked absolutely incapable of hurrying. I was mesmerised therefore, one afternoon, to find her running through the wood at an exceptionally lively rate, her usually white face pink with fright and exertion. The raven was after her, in full cry, charmed out of any semblance of phlegm by the impression he had made on his victim. He was tremendously excited by his conquest; the unfortunate

THE RAVEN

THE RAVEN LOOKS ON WHILE THE SHEEP-DOGS STEAL HIS DINNER

girl was unable to stir from the cottage door
the rest of her visit without some weapon of
defence.

The first time I passed a bed of azaleas I
thought I had found a new variety of spring-
flowering honeysuckle. The large golden-
cream or flame flowers were exactly like honeysuckle blooms, with an overpoweringly sweet
scent. I have learned since what they are,
that they like a heavy diet if they are to go
in thin hungry ground, and that the bulbs
to plant amongst them are the great lilium
auratum, the golden-rayed lily of Japan.
This combination gives us the scent and colour
of the azaleas in spring, and affords the
necessary protection to the lilies, which will
bloom from mid or late August well on into
the autumn. The azalea leaves turn bril-
liantly late in the year, and add greatly to the
colour scheme. Lilium auratum bulbs are
ready to plant in February or March, and like
some peat and leaf soil to root into. Once
they are planted, neither they nor the azalea
should be disturbed. They will go on for
years giving abundant bloom and increasing
in size and splendour.

A child set me a problem for a colour picture last autumn. We were talking garden talk. I said I was planning pretty colours to plant now, ready for spring time, and I went on rashly, " Tell me the prettiest thing you ever saw in a garden, and I will try to make it for you to see next April." The nearest he could get to what was evidently a very strong and beloved memory picture ran thus :—" A blue cloud it was, you know, all feathery blue, like a cloud, and it had bluer things in it like swords, you know, like blue swords they were." What flowers made this effect precisely I shall probably never know. Anyway, a long border is now planted thickly with forget-me-nots and Heavenly Blue muscari. In spring time I will bring the little man to see, and tell me if I have guessed near or far from what he wanted. In front of that same border is a long line of Her Majesty pinks. The sober silvery-grey of the foliage will tone excellently with the blues of the myosotis and muscari, especially as it leans on the cold blue-grey edge of a stone path. The combination is quite an experiment. I have never tried it before, nor heard of anyone else trying it. I think it will be very beautiful ; I did not get the very dwarf dark lobelia-blue myosotis, but the taller commoner pale blue variety, as I judge it will look better and be of a better height against the brilliant spikes of the muscari.

There is a certain tiny lawn between the house and the wood, flanked on one side by ivied walls and a lily-of-the-valley border ; opposite by a tiled path and rosemary hedge ; and on the third by a sombre bank of arbor vitæ. It is a cool green little spot, where we love to have meals in hot weather, but it lacked colour, and I debated long between a rhododendron bush and a bed of flowers. The bed won because it can be so much longer in bloom if carefully arranged. So first it was wedded to the Garden Beautiful with a broad gold ring of crocuses, and later, in May, it burned with bronze and scarlet tulips, till in autumn it is a fiery display of red-hot poker shafts, which are growing so healthily that they threaten to engulf the bed ; these plants need just such a background of gloomy green as they have there to make them noisily articulate in the garden scheme.

It is not everything that will grow under pines, so I am humbly grateful to find the beloved bluebells will thrive there, and make deep pools of blue under the hawthorn hedge which divides the little wood from the kitchen garden. True, I give them what chance I can, planting where the soil has been deeply dug throughout and the contents of several dustbins buried ; also I mix bone meal with the soil and sprinkle lightly sulphate of potash over the ground after the bulbs are in.

The front of the house was a bower of starry white clematis. I say " was " because I pruned it in the busybody days of ignorance. All unaware of the exceeding ticklishness of pruning clematis I hacked and hewed and ruined a lovely creeper, I fear, for ever. There are four or five different families of this plant and each one wants most particular knowledge in the pruning line. Regrets are weak and useless but they catch me from time to time as I look at the bare place the creeper used to make so beautiful ; it is not the usual large-flowered white Jackmanii, which blooms much later, but the early fast-growing Montana clematis, which gives you the feathery clusters

of traveller's joy in the autumn. I think it
is Miss Jekyll who talks about growing it in
combination with the guelder rose on a wall,
a scheme I would dearly like to try, but cannot, as I have no wall space to spare. The
great white snowballs of the guelder rose
follow close on the heels of lilac ; in fact, I
have them planted together for that reason,
and I can well conceive that its stiff decorative
quality would look exceedingly well with the
long white-starred sprays of the Montana
clematis flung about it. The snowballs are
a great joy in the house ; they look best cut
in generous boughs, and set in big Florentine
" brocchi," where their white globes are
reflected in a rosy metallic glow. It is a pity
laburnums do not keep indoors like the guelder
roses do, but then the snowballs and rhododendrons are peculiarly kind in water. I have
never been able to keep either wistaria or
laburnum long in the house. I think the
latter would be more extensively grown if
people knew how hardy and accommodating
it is in the matter of soil. In my youth we
had a drive planted entirely with them, and
the golden chains made a dazzling spectacle

indeed. To get colour effect it is essential to plant in masses ; many people have one of everything in their gardens and so in the sum total get nothing.

Having advocated a diary I may as well quote from mine to show my own rather cumbersome method of keeping pace with the flowers. I notice every year with fresh amusement how the race of bloom gets the better of me and the diary. There is profusion of comment, not to say garrulous comment, through spring, autumn and winter, but at the end of May remarks grow terse and businesslike, in June almost illegibly short and crowded, and through July and August a howling blank betrays the triumph of the garden over the study.

" *March* 16*th*, 1911. Snowdrops and chionodoxa bulbs now in bloom under the rosemary hedge, a thrilling stream of cold clear colour. The rock garden looks like a series of tiny lakes set in the grey stone pockets, varying in intensity of blue. Here and there one blue trickles over into another ; down near the bottom is a deep purple patch of Iris reticulata ; it has been blooming all through February. Above it is a late bloom of Iris alata, blossoming incessantly since November, interrupted seldom this mild winter by frost. In colour blue, and in form like a lovely orchid, big as a child's hand, it has a thin succulent flower-stem like a crocus, and luxuriant foliage. I only planted that patch of alata the first week in October.

"There is a dim blue break in the dark ground where the scillas and muscari are peeping. How blue the spring flowers are! Down there below the hedge at the end of the lawn are streaks of rusty yellow, where the aconites are going off; and on the mound below the rose garden, which is crowned with birch and pine trees, there are sheets of gold and purple crocuses. All along the grey stone of the terrace path, and in a broad strip under the study window, Baron von Brunow is out (a pale lavender blue crocus). Sir John Franklin (a large purple crocus) is big as many a tulip—in that thick patch by the summer-house he looks like a deep purple velvet cushion on a green carpet. All the garden brims with promise. The pigeons are carrying twigs to the dovecote, their cooing echoes through the pine trees. In a week or two colour will burst from every nook and corner of this little lovely garden.

"*March* 30*th*. That annoying japonica is in its full scarlet. I ought never to have let the carpenter give it to me. I tried to explain, in a timid way, that his pretty cottage in the valley was white and mine up there on the hill was red; but he did not understand, and I had no heart to stay his generous hands when they went fumbling to the roots of the little tree. So it was carried triumphantly up the lane and set against the red wall, where it blooms violently every spring. I go to look at it, fascinated by its spiteful vigour, as totally incapable of moving it as I am of turning the cottage white to do it justice. I don't like japonica on red walls.

"Here, against a sunny wall, is the thrice blessed yellow winter jasmine, the hardiest and least exacting of winter climbers. A frost comes along and tarnishes its gold, but the next mild spell finds it a sheet of yellow again, and so it persists.

"*April* 6*th*. I have been greatly exercised in mind about a little fellow on the rockery, so tiny, barely three inches high, yet what of him has been left by a slug or something proves him to be a perfect small daffodil. I found him in the lane last autumn, a lonely little bulb lying ready for the next foot to tread upon, so I took him home and put him in the rock garden for charity's sake. If he were less nibbled and more respectable I would send him off to be named; but I am too ashamed of him. Next year I will watch carefully against slugs and all other marauders, then learn his name, price, and habit, by sending a bloom to the bulb merchant, and if he is reasonably cheap, plant a whole pocketful there, for he is adorable. In my inmost heart I suspect him of being 'Minimus,' especially as he has bloomed so early.

"*April 27th. How* the daffodils are blooming! There are golden sheets and starry clusters in every shady reach. On the mound at the end of the rose garden, where the crocuses are gathering strength from their flowerless leaves to bloom next year, the cowslips are out; they curse me with their pale little faces for not giving them deep rich pasture-land to grow on, but how can I on a sandy hill ? In the new orchard at the bottom of the kitchen garden cherry and pear and plum are a frothy mass of white bloom. Through the pine wood the wind brings a sweet warm breath of perfume every now and then ; it comes from the dells where pheasant's-eye narcissus have been naturalised, and where they busy themselves with scenting every breeze that passes near. The border under the terrace is a gorgeous ribbon of flame-colour ; it flashes on the eye at intervals as one comes through the wood, and then bursts into full view as one comes into the iris garden, a dazzling ribbon of orange and yellow. It is made of blood-red wallflowers, Thomas Moore tulips, and Pottebakkar yellow tulips. The clear deep yellow of the last leads easily into the rich orange of Thomas Moore, and culminates in the intense red of the wallflowers.

"1911, *May* (*2nd week*). Nasty gap in flowering. *Note:* Get late Darwin tulips for another year."

Looking at an early May entry for 1912, I find :—

"Beyond the rock garden with its many patches of warm purple aubretia and cold clear blue muscari is a brilliant display of gesneriana major (late scarlet tulips). They seem to echo and accentuate the note struck faintly in early April by the Duc van Thol dwarfs."

So the note was evidently faithfully read and profited by.

"*April*, 1912. Went to Old Kiln to-day and saw the new deep lobelia-coloured forget-me-not in masses. It grows low. I stole a spray, and tried it with Dr. Mules Aubretia. *Note:* Plant them together on rockery or along a border. Too brilliant to be missed.

"*May 2nd*, 1912. Ivory white tulips and golden wallflowers are more refined and less tiring than the old blood-red wallflowers and yellow and flame tulip idea. Also fewer people have thought of it. Might try it again.

"*October 18th*. I have been watching the trees. I wish I could give the space of the kitchen garden to trees; a whole range of delightful effects would be secured in autumn against the sombre background of the pines—

Juniper with its grey-green foliage, holly, thorns, which go so warmly ruddy, scotch fir, birch, medlar, quince and wild guelder rose, would make beautiful and harmonious colour.

" *Note :* Aster amellus is invaluable, low, and more manageable than the taller variety. Get a range of colour for the front terrace beds.

" *January 2nd.* Friends who love their gardens and are keenly sensitive to the moods of nature tell me how they notice the change in the tree sounds at this time of the year. The wind, instead of rustling through branches thick with leaves, instead of pushing full-throated through the multitudinous summer foliage, whistles reedily through bare boughs, scraping and screaming where before it pushed and purred. And then I tell them of the wind noises in my garden, which are the same all the year round because the wood is a pine wood : of how the wind stirs there with a rhythmic monotony, just like the sea breaking on a stony shore, rougher at the equinoxes, but otherwise varying not at all. I lean from the window and can hear day and night, all the year round, that dreadful and fascinating sound."

And so the diary goes babbling on—a useful gossipy busybody book.

CHAPTER IV

THE DOVECOTE

I NEVER knew, when I lived in cities, that pigeons were one of the needs of a garden. I saw, and admired often, as we all do, the fat blue-grey smut-stained fellows which used to steal corn from the horses' nosebags in the Temple and round the British Museum and Guildhall, but somehow I never associated them with gardens— only with an old grey city. It was after I had had a garden for some time that a stray pigeon alighted on the bedroom window one morning. First I heard the sharp, acid swish of wings, and then the scratch of little feet on an open casement. I lay very still and watched. It was a big pigeon; presently he threw his chest out and cooed. As he cooed, I could see in fancy a white flock of these pretty creatures flying against the sombre velvety background of pines, could see the glisten of white wings in the sun, and feel how good it would be to hear the swish of them every morning among the murmurs of the trees. The idea germinated slowly ; it only burst into full life one day when I saw mine host at the inn in the valley rolling a handsome barrel into the back yard. " It would look nice on a pole and cut into pigeon lockers," I thought.

So the village carpenter was called in, and the brandy barrel was cut into very fine lockers with ledges, and a noble roof, capped with lead, was designed for it. It became a joyous pilgrimage after tea on an afternoon to go down the valley and " see how the dove-cote was getting on." It was painted cream. A straight young pine was tarred at the base, and one day the dovecote was borne in triumph to the cottage on the hill, mounted on the pole, and planted in full view of the house against a background of pines. So far, so good. It was exceedingly decorative, and cost very little. Then I had to leave home for Canada, and it occurred to me that I should like to find a flourishing colony of

white pigeons fulfilling their ornamental purpose when I returned. So I left instructions with the Master that a couple of pairs
of fantails should be bought and induced to
stay. He, poor soul, having a pathetic
belief in the domestic virtues of pigeons, was
induced to vary my instructions to the extent
of installing a pair of fantails and a pair of
magpie pigeons, a black and white hen, and
a brown and white cock-bird. Now fantails,
as we all know, have puffed-out chests and
tails which are lifted and spread out like
a fan. Chubby, consequential, self-satisfied
birds they are. Magpies are the direct opposite : long, slim, elegant creatures, whose
beauty depends very much on their high-
bred figures and the exactness of their mark-
ing. The last two varieties in the world one
would think of mixing.

The splendour of their quarters made the
fantails at once inordinately proud, and it
was then (having got over the shock of seeing
the mixed varieties) that we made the pleasing
discovery that the " pair " of fantails were
both gentlemen, and that the black and
white magpie was the worried recipient of

advances from all the others—the two ineligibles, and a frightened meek magpie husband. To cut a disgraceful story short, she finally accepted the bigger fantail, who was an awful bully. (Horrible mixtures the young pigeons were—dreadful—impossibly ugly.) The other fantail emigrated, and settled himself at the " Spotted Cow " in the valley with a wife he found somewhere. But the poor little brown and white magpie never got over his disappointment. He would sit miserably watching his erring spouse, forgiving her, and entreating her (when her bully of a lover was not about) to come back to him. Maternity adorned that bird : she was never so pretty nor so happy as when sitting on her white eggs or rearing a family. It used to grieve me to the core when lost in admiration of her to reflect that she was wasting all that beauty of devotion on a scoundrel and ugly children. There came a day, about a year after her elopement, when the little brown and white pigeon moped and refused to eat. Believing him to be dying of a broken heart, I ordered every single pigeon except him and his former spouse to be shot. The ugly young squabs made a very good pie. The old fantail was tough.

Then for a halcyon moon that devoted brown magpie was happy. He crammed enough of ecstasy into his cooing to assuage the grief of the widow and make himself and his message into a sort of incessant heartbeat through the pines. Day and day on, from earliest light, I would hear the little enraptured throat persuading and admiring and adoring. In the deepest night one would hear from the dovecote a faint throbbing coo ; and one knew how he had waked in terror lest it was all a dream, and feeling her within reach, had nestled closer and cooed himself to joyous sleep again. He was so happy that he radiated delight through the garden. We never ceased to love watching his tender fussing ; and the day the little hen was seen carrying twigs of heather to a locker marked an epoch. Everybody in the house told everyone else that the " pigeons were building—wasn't it jolly ? " The love story of the brown gentleman had made a great appeal.

One morning we found him moping on his perch with his feathers ruffled back and dull eyes. And then we discovered that the little lady was missing. Goodness knows what happened to her. She must have been snared or shot, for she was much too devoted to domesticity to leave home of her own accord; unless she met the other fantail, and mistook him for the first—in which case she was a hussy, and I have no patience with her.

We killed the poor little suffering lover for pity's sake.

It was quite a time before I could face the pigeon business again. It was a revelation to learn that birds had so much character. When finally a longing for the sound of cooing in the wood grew stronger than pity, I started to remedy an error we had discovered in the first dovecote. It was too small. So a successor was made out of a bigger barrel, cut into twice as many lockers, and bravely thatched with heather. It stands in the place of the first, painted cream, as the other was, set up on a stout pine shaft, making a very noticeable and effective feature in the garden.

Then ensued a long and painful period of

despair, all owing to the kindness of a neighbour. She knew the lamentable tale of the first effort, and when she heard another dovecote was erected she made a generous gift of some young birds from her own pretty but heterogeneous flock to go in it, and the obstinate creatures (in whose veins I now fancy must flow a strong strain of Homer blood) would appear on the lawn with the utmost method at feeding time but would neither adorn my loft nor breed in it. I got tired when I found they bred and lived in their old home and only came to me for food, so I went to friend Gamage again and bought tumblers this time ; I thought they would entertain us in the summer evenings with their quaint aerial antics—they were pretty birds and there was a flutter in the household at their installation. It was then I learned what a serpent I had nourished in my bosom when I accepted my neighbour's young birds, who came, as ever, with the most perfect regularity at feeding time, and decoyed my tumblers to their own more spacious quarters ! I told the neighbour of my hard case, and she was as distressed as the occasion warranted, offering me any number of young birds to make up, and deploring with me the inscrutable ways of Providence in endowing pigeons with such mulish natures.

However, I pointed out to her that the remedy hardly lay in my accepting any *more* of her birds, kind though the offer was, and for many a month the grand new dovecote stood desolate in its pride, a reproach to my ignorance of bird-craft.

Then one day Fate looked my way again. A cottage in the valley being over-endowed with babes and under-endowed with pence took to itself a gun and shot my neighbour's birds, so that they ceased to mock me every morning, coming for food and leaving directly after. Hope revived and I thought I might try again ; but to make assurance doubly sure I determined to breed a few pairs in captivity before releasing any. Being away from the cottage I spent an evening designing a light structure of bamboo and wire to go over the whole of the dovecote, and sent it to the gardener for local construction. I reckoned it would cost about 30s. or £2. Hearing in due course that it was ready I suggested running down to the cottage with the Master, as I had a surprise for him. I believe he was very surprised. I know I was. A magnificent palace of fine proportions, an aviary, in short, like the eagle-house at the Zoo, or such as a millionaire might order, had grown out of my harmless little sketch. We walked round it, dazed and unbelieving ; and all the comment I could get from my astonished comrade was " pigeons ought to do well there."

As a matter of fact, they have done very well indeed ; I have now a large thorough-bred flock of black and white magpie pigeons.

That first little hen bird I ever had made a great impression on me as a mother, and I found the black and whites were less expensive to start with than the brown and white, though sentiment made one lean strongly to the latter. Magpies are a fancy variety, and the young pairs will sell at about 5s. to 6s. a pair, which makes them profitable in time. The slim graceful line of the creatures pleases me more than the bombastic outline of fantails, and their cooing is much softer and sweeter—a great consideration if they are to be kept near the house. A flock of

fantails can wake a household very early in
the morning with their loud voices.

To anyone who has space—and most
gardens have it—a dovecote is a charming
thing, and inexpensive too. It can easily be
home-made, and one pair of birds will soon
people it, with occasional introductions of
fresh stock, of course, to prevent undue
inbreeding.

It is wise to keep the first pair shut up for
a year, or six months at least, till they have
bred several young ones. Then, even if the
old birds return to their old home on libera-
tion, those bred in the home loft will remain
and go on increasing. While they are in
captivity it is important to give them a good
bowl of mixed salt, lime, and grit to peck at ;
it makes all the difference in their health and
in the number of birds that will hatch out.
I collect all the mortar rubble and masons'
rubbish I can find when workmen are busy
about house or garden, and keep it in a cupboard in the study (which the Master
says is full of untidiness). Then, when I
find their stock is running low, I get some
of the sand washed by the brook in the valley,

and mix it with the squashed rubble and kitchen salt, and refill. A fair substitute is a cake of " Tipcat " sold especially for pigeons, which tastes salt and smells of aniseed, though I cannot say for certain what else it contains. They are very fond of it and will peck at it for hours.

It is wise to keep the birds well in mind, and when the hen has laid her first egg remove it for a day or two, till she has laid the second. Then replace it at once, so that she may sit on the two simultaneously, otherwise she will start sitting at once, and one of the younger birds will be so much bigger and stronger than the other, being hatched a couple of days earlier, that he will get more than his share of food, and probably end by pushing his brother out of the nest and killing him.

The young ones grow very rapidly. It is a grand sight to see a flock of well-bred pigeons planing down in the sunset, or walking about the garden with all the iridescence of the peacock glancing along their supple throats. They walk with a pretty strut, and grow very tame if fed always by the same hand ; it is a source of unending amusement and interest to have them in sight of the house and watch their ardent busy little lives and varying temperaments. I should be very sorry to miss them from the garden now; though, as in everything else, I started off in happiest ignorance, and have achieved my little success through the interesting if devious paths of experience.

CHAPTER V

THE ROSE GARDEN

NO one could really have started rose-growing in more perfect ignorance than I. Looking at the sandy desert which surrounded the cottage four years ago, I bethought me that roses climbing and scrambling everywhere would be a pleasant change, so I walked off across country, through hopfields, to a nursery I had heard of, in order to collect some rose trees. It was with surprise I learned that July was not the best month in which to transplant things from the open, and that if I really must have roses at once, to bloom at once, they must be roses out of pots. Four was all I thought I could carry at that rate ; and it will be long before I forget the toilsome return over the interminable hopfields carrying four hefty flower-pots. Nor will I readily forget the planting of them :

a little hole dug in the dry hot sand, the plant turned out of its pot, put in, and then well watered in the blazing sun with a good can of ice cold water off the main. Every error the willing fool can commit I made in planting my victims. A highly unsuccessful rose harvest, coupled with some glimpses of other people's roseries, led me to buy Dean Hole's book on roses, and there I learned the fatal glibness of the early endeavour. Soon I knew enough to envy with all my heart and soul those lucky folk who have a rich loamy soil over clay, where roses cannot *help* growing if the drainage is sound. They never grow well where their roots are waterlogged. The drainage in my garden is excellent but everything else is wrong.

Goodness knows there was enough to learn ! First I was told to dig a good deep hole, to fill this in with manure, and then loam. Then I had to learn that scamping is no good ; that that " good deep hole " must be at least three feet deep and as many wide. And then, through slow observation, I have grown to entertain a personal and divergent opinion as to the bottom layer of manure ; I believe it is a mistake in such thin soil as mine. It is wiser, I believe, to fill in entirely with loam, then plant the rose well, with the roots spread carefully round, and to top dress liberally with good farmyard manure. This method encourages surface-rooting, which is all to be commended when deep-rooting will only discover sand and gravel ; watering with liquid manure when the buds are forming is a great help, too, in the same direction. Taking things all round I think the best tip is the one I have only recently had given me, and that is, to grow roses on their own roots. It is not a tip for everyone, of course, only for gardeners on such soil as this. Another idea I firmly adhere to is that basic slag is a grand aid to rose-growing in a light soil. I always apply it in the autumn, as it is a slow-acting phosphatic manure ; the effects of it are plain in spring, after the heavy autumn and winter rains have washed it well down.

To revert to the matter of the " good deep hole." It is no use being mean about it; a small hole—any hole less than I have mentioned —is useless. For the reward that awaits the sincere gardener it is worth while to endure some more of backache and dig out really deep; it is better to plant one rose bush well than a dozen scurvily. The roots prefer not to be crammed in; they like to be spread out patiently and carefully, as they then withstand better the up-tearing gales of the equinoxes; the wide grip gives the roots a better purchase on the soil. It is wise to prune any root, before planting, of the long suckers which are no use and only exhaust the plant; they are readily distinguished from the roots proper because they have no fibre on them. It is the hairy fibres that matter on a root.

If one has space for it, I think it is a good plan to devote a place apart for a rose garden, however small; and some people go so far as to treat everything in that space which is not a rose as a weed. For one thing it keeps the rose-labour well together, a great help when syringing, mulching and pruning times are afoot; for another, the rose is so lovely a medium that it lends itself to special treatment, and the clever informal formality of modern rose gardens is exceedingly beautiful.

H

When Turner brought out the Crimson Rambler rose he revolutionised the ideas of gardeners. From prim stiff standard trees in rows and beds it is a far cry to the tangling froth and feather of the rambler and its varieties. I cannot picture a rose garden of to-day which has its lines unbroken by these lawless happy-go-lucky fellows. They are such Bohemians, so impatient of restraint, so eager, so effective. They give an air of hospitable informality to every garden they have found their place within, and I love them for their wild loveliness just as dearly as I admire the order and the rhythm of the disciplined habit of the H. P. roses—the tidy grace of these latter, their restrained effects, their culture and breed, and air of it all! They are as humorous in their niggardliness and self-esteem as the ramblers are in their vigorous extravagance of growth. The tea roses are the adorable mean ; they are neither prim nor stiff, nor are they boisterous and ambitious, but trail their part through the comedy of the rose garden with wonderful self-possession. Just enough to hint at freedom they give us of their glorious sprays, just enough to tell of breed they have in the comely order of their blooms.

I, personally, lean to a flagged sunk garden, in some sheltered chosen spot, with surrounding clipped yew hedges to give intensity of background, and a clear jet of water playing from a fountain in the centre. It is the ideal which glows far off and always grows lovelier with thinking on: formal box-edged beds, each bedded with its one variety of rose, saved from monotony by frequent arches and pillars. In dreams I can see the petals, white and gold and scarlet and rose, driven along the grey flagstones into scented heaps under the small neat box edging ; and heaven knows which is the more delightful—the having or the dreaming. I expect most people have their perfect vision and second best reality.

Of all the gardens in a garden devoted to roses, surely mine is the smallest, and none in all the world can give such exquisite joy as mine to me. It has twelve beds only, four arches, a row of pillar roses, and a tiny flagged centre circle with four tiled paths radiating away from it ; yet for all its unpretentious design the rose garden is very beautiful, especially when the carmine pillars are out in long shafts of intense red. At a distance the brilliant single bloom is like a geranium, a suggestion that always repeats itself a little later, when the Hiawatha weepers come along with their great trusses of single scarlet.

I must confess I have never really mastered the art of pruning. It is indeed an extremely complicated science. The H. P. roses want cutting hard, I am told, and the H. T. more leniently; so far, so good. In early spring behold me going out armed with secateurs to hover miserably about the bushes. What *is* "hard"? What *is* "lenient" cutting? Then again, which are Hybrid Perpetual varieties? Which Hybrid Teas? I go and consult my staunch friend and ally the gardener; he looks on me with sympathy and says it's hard to know. Then I leave the wild March weather and go indoors to consult friend Hole, and friend Biron in the *Gardener*. Later I return to the fray refreshed with knowledge; I know the H. P. from the H. T. Then once again the busy tormenting brain bites at my hand and stops the secateurs. What *is* "hard"? What *is* "lenient"? I always end by delivering the beds into the hands of the gardener, who has long deserted the intricacies of modern rose-lore, preserving an amiable uniformity of method. He pares the beds to one height throughout and is content.

One variety I have no hesitation about. As soon as the ramblers have finished blooming I go round in autumn and ruthlessly cut away *all* the old wood ; one can afford to be very stern about it on this light soil. Only the young wood is allowed to bloom next year, and I have never regretted the system. The bloom is fine and strong, and I am convinced that the real secret of success lies in that relentless pruning after bloom time.

After the spring pruning, the next job in the rose garden is syringing the green fly. In my youth measles was supposed to be an essential part of human development, and when I started rose growing I took it as a matter of course that every rose bush should harbour green fly and be treated accordingly. Nowadays certain sturdy reformers go round saying that no child need have measles, that it is quite unnecessary, indeed it is only a form of dirt (being a disease, and all disease being dirt); and rose-growers of the most modern school will tell one that a healthy rose tree never has green fly; so my treatment varies entirely with my mood. Some days I go into the rose garden filled with so hearty a belief in the goodness of Nature that I hardly believe I can spy a green fly anywhere, and all is well. On other days I go round in moody wise, discover plentiful evidence of the pest, and hurriedly collect soft-soap, rain-water, and the big brass syringe to combat the enemy. Other days I will slink through the garden with averted head, filled with shame at the very thought that some of my rose trees may be so ill-nourished and unhealthy as to carry damning evidence of the same green fly.

I must confess that the more vigorous roses like Frau Karl Druschki and Mme. A. M. Kirker are comparatively free, while the more delicate Hybrid Teas like Lady Hillingdon and Irish Elegance are very liable to green fly. It may be of interest to other owners of sandy gardens if I here make mention of the roses that I find by experience grow well in my own little rose-patch. One great favourite is Robert Craig, and somehow or other I have never seen it in any other private garden but mine. It is an exceedingly vigorous climber with extraordinary foliage of red-brown in the young shoots, and glossy as if each leaf had been varnished or richly glazed. It blooms with a very pretty habit, so that one can cut long sprays for indoors; and so profuse is it that I can fill the parlour, and the tree looks none the poorer for the cutting. The buds are of fine copper yellow like William Allan Richardson; as the flowers open they turn creamier and sometimes end up snow-white, so that the varying shades on one spray are exceedingly beautiful. The flower, not the leaf, has a very sweet scent like the strongest sweetbriar.

Another rose I use extensively as a pillar is Hiawatha. It has a persistent habit of taking a long time to establish itself. Every time I plant a Hiawatha I know that I shall have to wait till the third summer to see any really fine display. Madame Alfred Carriere is a rather straggly climber but blooms with a good heart from early summer till very late in the autumn, almost to Christmas; she carries long stalks and large loose blooms of a low-toned warm white with dainty appealing perfume. I find the Goldfinch a vigorous and not to say boisterous rambler ; it grows with great rapidity, throwing up immense canes every season, and it blooms in large trusses of single copper turning to white. One virtue about it is that it beats even the little old-fashioned Garland for heavy honey-sweetness of scent. On a summer morning when the Goldfinch arch is in full bloom, and when there has been a little rain in the night, it is a distinct sensuous joy to pass by, and wind the musk in it, sweet and indolent and voluptuous, not at all like the frail pure perfume of Madame A. Carriere.

A rambler I can recommend with all my heart is Tausendschön ; it should become an inveterate favourite ; maybe it is now, for all I know. It has a very long bloom time, and is a vigorous grower, carrying flowers like Dorothy Perkins—not that hard pink, but of a very soft pink and much larger flowers. It is practically thornless, comes into bloom early, and throws out second and sometimes even third relays very grateful and com-

THE FIRST ARCH WE PUT UP

THE SAME ARCH TWO YEARS LATER COVERED WITH A RAMBLING ROSE

forting to the eye. If anyone grows roses in the herbaceous borders I would recommend pillars of Tausendschön grown among the great spikes of blue delphiniums. The effect is very good. I prefer the warm pink to the much vaunted and often copied Madonna lily and delphinium combination. A brilliant orange or a warm rose colour is infinitely more to my taste among delphiniums.

When I first started gardening, one of the friends who most hotly advocates the aforesaid delphinium-Madonna-lily combination told me to plant Dorothy Perkins next to a purple clematis, as the colours were effective together and the bloom time synchronised. So behold me, full of gratitude, enthusiasm, and ignorance, spanning the path from the entrance gate to the house with two arches, the one planted with Dorothy, the other with purple Jackmanni clematis. Both arches have thriven exceedingly, and every July I am rent with the same desire to uproot the purple clematis and plant a red Jackmanni in its place. The red would look fine, indeed, leading on to the dominant noisy pink of the Dorothy arch. The purple is too blue, too strident, and I dislike the combination very much. But every autumn when I ought to make the change I hesitate and let the moment go, for clematis, although a hardy climber, is a very uncertain thing to grow, and when a plant has taken good and certain hold of any spot it is as well to be grateful and let it be.

So there it is, and so much for other people's advice. One has to learn for oneself to please oneself.

The four big circular beds which make the heart of my rose garden design, carry respectively Frau Karl Druschki, Madame A. M. Kirker, Caroline Testout, and Richmond. These are all vigorous growers. Frau Karl is indeed a miracle, growing rampantly like a vigorous forest tree, and blooming with joyous open-hearted generosity all along the shoots. I do not know of any rose of such perfect shape ; and the hard waxy white is too well known to need description. I fill my arm with blooms from the Frau Karl bed, and fill the house and send boxes to my friends, and still the bed is amply furnished.

Every rose seems to have a failing. Frau

Karl has no scent and Madame A. M. Kirker
(which I reckon next to Frau Karl as a
success on my soil), although she grows
vigorously, blooms so freely and so late into
the autumn, although her bright rose-coloured
blooms are of magnificent shape and texture,
although her scent is rich and powerful, has
the ugly failing of turning purple when plucked
and put into vases. She loses colour too,
and turns purple after rain if allowed to
wither on the bush. Caroline Testout, the
fine large salmon-pink and almost scentless
rose, is keen, vigorous, and well liking; on
one of the arches I had a climber of this
variety and it sent up a shoot eight feet
high in one season. The bed of Richmond
is generally well filled with bloom. It is a
good rose. I do not speak so warmly of it
as perhaps I should—other growers seem
to be much more enthusiastic about it. I
have seen it when it left nothing to be
desired. It is a rose one must be careful to
disbud, like Grüss An Teplitz. It is so free
that it will give one a multitude of ineffective
blooms unless a very large proportion of the
buds are destroyed.

I have other beds. One, very lovely, is circular in shape, edged all round with the little white Scotch rose, which blooms like a mass of snow and smells of sweetbriar ; in the centre are tall bushes of the wonderful Austrian Copper briar with its single flowers of marvellous far-reaching flame colour, the colour indeed of nasturtiums ; the rest of the bed, which is a large one, is planted out with the new rose Juliet, a cross between Captain Hayward and the rich coloured Soleil d'Or. Juliet has a peculiar individual perfume, strong and invigorating. The flowers are very large, of a strange yellow pink, a colour once seen never forgotten—a kind of exaggerated salmon apricot, the most curious hybrid, I should say, of modern years. The growth is rather straggly and briar-like. Juliet is the extraordinary product of a most unnatural union. I sigh with sympathy when I think of poor Captain Hayward, the shapely tidy-living nicely bred gentleman that he is, wedded to that wild gipsy Soleil d'Or with her unmistakable briar habit and straggling impossible growth. It must have been a most uncomfortable, not to say discordant ménage !

I grow Juliet more, I believe, from an amazed interest than any other motive. I see the distinct features of either parent so strongly marked, so crudely united, in their wayward beautiful bizarre daughter.

A bed of which I am well proud is the yellow bed where Lady Hillingdon, the aristocratic beauty, breathing high blood in every line of her, blooms from early summer till nearly Christmas. She is a comparatively new rose, and very precious. The foliage is a deep reddish-brown, the growth free ; the blooms, which are plentiful, of a clear deep apricot, very long and shapely. When open fully the petals have a careless grace, a fine engaging abandon, not the faintest degree blowsy, but very free. The only fault I find is that vases containing blooms must stand high on a piano or bracket, or some place above the eye level, as they hang down like Maréchal Neil roses.

The bed of Mrs. Longworth is one of which I am also very proud, and have never seen in any other garden. I wonder this rose is not better known. She was raised by Prince, of Oxford, and reminds me more than anything

else of the form of the new beautiful pæonies
—the wide curly petal of dainty creamy
white, splashed and streaked with frail pink.
A characteristic is the gloss on the underside
of each petal ; velvety soft on the inner side,
it has that china bright glaze on the outer
petal, giving a waxen beauty to the half
unfolded blooms. It grows freely, is beautiful in every stage, with a very refined perfume
exactly like the smell of a wild rose, and is
very beautiful for indoor decoration.

The most pleasing Hybrid Tea with single
blooms I used to consider Irish Elegance,
and I had a bed of the deep copper orange
flowers which open to the colour of our old
friend Gloire de Dijon. I found, however,
that for all its beauty it mildewed easily and
grew rather straggly, so that when my friend
Mr. Bide, the indefatigable rose expert of
Farnham, gave me one day a bunch of his
Mrs. W. T. Massey, which he said was in
every way a very much better Irish Elegance,
I ordered a bed to try it. It has endorsed all
he claimed, to my great satisfaction. I should
strongly advocate Mrs. W. T. Massey in place
of Irish Elegance.

Four other little beds complete the tale of my tiny rose garden, each planted in the centre with a standard Madame Abel Chatenay, that most wonderful and indispensable rose. I suppose none is better known on the London market. The salmon pink with the silvery reflex, the curly petal, the long shapely bloom, the freedom and the beauty of it—who does not know Madame Chatenay ?

These beds, which are round, are carpeted with the little velvet dwarf polyantha ; one with the new Jessie, the brightest purest scarlet of any of this variety. It makes a dazzling carpet of colour, seems totally impervious to rain and merrily to love the sun. Another is bedded with Orleans, a little pink polyantha ; another with Madame Norbert Levavasseur, which, like most polyantha roses, blooms persistently late in the autumn ; the only trouble I have with this variety is its ugly habit of turning purple. The new sport from this rose is Erna Teschendorf, and is said to resemble Madame Norbert Levavasseur in habit of growth and foliage. The flowers are of a deep carmine red colour, resembling Grüss An Teplitz. The single

blooms are fuller than those of Madame Norbert Levavasseur, and this variety neither
loses its colour in the hottest sun, nor has
it any purple shades. It has received many
awards on the Continent and is said to be the
darkest polyantha rose in existence. The
other bed is filled with Annie Müller, the well-
known pink.

In other parts of the garden I have other
roses, of course ; some are young plants I have
not yet seen, and am looking forward to seeing
next summer : Lady Waterlow, for instance,
a strong and well spoken of climber ; Leontine
Gervais, a beautiful apricot climber; and
Silver Moon, the new single white climber.
In a very shady place, under a hot wall, are
Fortune's Yellow, Rosa Sinica Anemone, and
Maréchal Neil ; as the wall is only just made
and the plants are young, I have yet to learn
how the site will please them ; but, theoreti-
cally, for such tender varieties it is ideal.

Last year I tested Alice de Rothschild,
which proved a very strong grower, inclined
to mildew, and flat in the flower like Gloire de
Dijon, but a sweet and sturdy rose. Rayon
d'Or is a gem ; brilliant yellow, very shapely

THE TURFED ROSE-GARDEN IN JUNE-TIME

THE ROSE-GARDEN IN WINTER, FLAGGED AS IT IS NOW

in the bud, and strong, not to say rude, of growth. Natalie Bottner, the " yellow Frau Karl," has to prove herself. A climber to which I have devoted much attention is one Anna Rubsamen ; although not a very striking little rose at first sight it is so individual in temperament that it has an intimate way of becoming part of the garden, and safe lodged in one's esteem. It is a little capricious, perhaps, but, generally speaking, strong in growth, and bears large coral pink blooms of the Tausendschön shape and size, with an undying industry all through the summer and autumn ; I always like a rose that does its work with a good heart. This particular one is extremely difficult to obtain, in fact, all the plants I have ever known of it have come from one man who obtained it originally from a Stock Exchange acquaintance, and he admires it so much that he is always striking cuttings and giving them away to his friends. One of the loveliest arches I ever saw had this rose roaming freely among the deep red trusses of Crimson Rambler.

A bush of which I am very fond, but of which I do not know the name, is one bought from a neighbouring cottager ; it has a great flower, a rather flat-edged petal, is striped pink and red, and has a rich musky scent. It is probably some well-known old-fashioned variety. I do not know why one sees so seldom that thrice-blessed dearly-loved Conrad F. Meyer; perhaps the savage thorns are enough to prevent people growing him. There is always a race in first flowering between Conrad F. Meyer and Carmine Pillar, and generally Conrad wins. The bloom is an exquisite silvery pink, the shape and substance good ; the perfume brims out of him into the summer garden, an overwhelming luscious real rose perfume. The latest rose I bring into the house in the last days of autumn is frequently a Conrad F. Meyer— there seems no end to his energy and good will; as soon as one crop is over, another is in bud. I have learned better than to keep it in the rose garden, however ; its growth is too vigorous for the prim beds, the long thorny arms straggle in all directions, and tear the petals of more delicate sisters with every puff of wind, so Conrad has a place to himself in the kitchen garden, where he can grow into as big a bush as he wishes, and flower to his heart's content. There is Wichuriana blood in him, which accounts for the vigorous growth, and also suggests to the intelligent gardener that severe pruning is not indicated.

Commander Jules Gravereaux has been accorded quite an undue amount of interest, for he is a new variety and from his parentage I hoped great things of him. He is a cross from Richmond, the sweet-scented fine red, and Frau Karl Druschki, the loveliest white of to-day. Now, scent is the only virtue Frau Karl lacks, as I have already said, so the excitement of hearing there was a red Frau Karl with a sweet scent on the market was very great. I sent to France for enough bushes to fill a bed, and laboured over them with exceeding devotion.

Never did any rose less resemble Frau Karl. But I admire it. The blooms are like great single pæonies, excellent for bedding effect, the colour a clear brilliant blood-scarlet, and the scent charming, the habit of growth strong and promising. Each petal has a pinked edge. It has a large handsome loose, very effective bloom, with a wide crown of golden anthers, and I like it very much. The shoots flower singly like Madame Alfred Carriere, and do not need disbudding, as Frau Karl does.

When I can spare time I like to walk over the fields, that same old never-to-be-forgotten walk across the hopfields to Mr. Bide's nurseries, where I bought my first roses in pots ; then if I find him in a kindly mood, with time to spare, we ramble through the acres of blooming roses and talk over the new varieties ; or his hybridising expert will take me through the long greenhouse and show me seedling plants of new varieties. Nothing fascinates me more than this branch of rose culture. When I was on the Canadian prairies I took great heed of the beautiful wild prairie rose, a low growing variety, very sweet-scented, ranging in the colour of its single blooms from rosy crimson to white. It grows about a foot high, and it occurred to me that the rose which could stand the prairie winters would probably yield to rose breeders in England some crossbred variety that would take them far along the path every nurseryman is trying to tread to-day. I mean the path leading them to the rose which will bloom throughout the winter, carrying the bloom-time of roses till roses come again.

Rose breeders are working very hard on the lines of late blooming varieties, and the heart of every gardener goes with them. At present the ramblers are very disappointing in continuity. They are a glorious sight when out, but in the vast majority of cases they pass completely, unlike the Hybrid Teas, which go on merrily till the hard frosts come. In pursuance of this brilliant inspiration, therefore, I brought home some seed pods of prairie roses and took them to friend Bide to experiment upon. Not in a single instance did one of the seeds germinate, and so, most unluckily, our experiment was a failure. Next time I go to Canada I shall try again, because I still believe that the habit of withstanding frost in any rose which can bloom on the Canadian prairie year after year must be so settled that with judicious crossing with some of our most persistent bloomers good results might be obtained.

One of the newest roses on the market is Lady Katherine Rose, a direct cross between

Antoine Rivoire and La Fraicheur. The colour of this rose is the same delicate pink as La Fraicheur, with those same unique markings in the petal which are characteristic of this beautiful rose; it radiates, too, its delicate scent. The growth, however, is identical with the seed parent, and the blooms are produced very freely on stout erect stems.

I hate to stop talking about roses, they are the loveliest and the dearest flowers of all in the garden. With the passing of them I always feel that indeed the year is growing to an end.

Looking down the garden diary, I see an entry for mid-July.

"The whole house is a bower of white roses—'Maids of the Village' they call them here—and when the petals fall they make a summer snowfall very sweet to smell. The arches are flushed with pink ramblers in full bloom, and the masterful crimson rambler has thrown great arms about the 'Maids of the Village' at the end of the terrace. The honeysuckle by the summer-house is making the butterflies drunk."

It breathes so warmly that I feel again in reading it what I have often felt, that there is something blatant about full summer ; the half-tones of spring and autumn are infinitely more precious.   The grey-rose of the evenings, the moist sweetness of the winds, the folding of the leaves to winter, the falling petals, the heavy seed-pods, the garnered grain, the tragic autumnal winds—all these have a profounder appeal than the hard, unclouded magnificence of summer.   I am never sorry to see comely autumn striding down the days. There are merry hours ahead, when we go with baskets gathering nuts and blackberries, hours unforgettable among the English hedges, where thorns take toll of our hands, and " old man's beard " tangles in our hair.

CHAPTER VI

ALL-THE-YEAR-ROUND stocks are fine, bushy plants, less "leggy" than the Bromptons, and are a cross between the Brompton and the " ten-week." They are only to be had in snow-white as yet. I wish there were bright scarlet and deep purple colours in them, when they would entirely supersede the untrustworthy Bromptons. The foliage is glossy, and the stems carry huge heads of pure white, very fragrant double flowers. The rascally Bromptons played the garden a low trick this year ; I had them massed in the herbaceous border to bloom instead of Darwin tulips (as they are so much cheaper than bulbs), and they went down under the frost like moon-daisies under a scythe ; so there was none of the glowing mass of pink and purple and crimson which I had pictured for those beds. The best beloved, the dearest and the most precious variety of all stocks, is the pale insignificant straggly night scented-stock growing beside the terrace path.

Look at it ! Flimsy of texture, poor in form, untidy in growth, unimportant in its gown of washed-out lilac. With the sun full overhead it shrinks almost to nothing, and looks like some shamed weed trying to escape notice. People are even apologetic for it as they go round the garden ; they turn and pretend not to see it, and pass on and ignore it. After dinner, in sunset time, when they are playing bridge or having coffee, or talking of the country, I go privily to that ragged patch, and, lo ! a miracle. The tiny pale flowers have opened wide and starry. In the first glimmering moonray their paleness shines luminous, and from them comes a wonderful scent.

All through the summer twilight that incense is flung to the stars. Night moths hang about it. It drifts with stray breezes to far corners of the garden and assails the exalted imaginations of lovers with visions of instant paradise. Very few people trace it to its source. They breathe it, write dreamy impressionist poems to it, improvise music to it, and, generally speaking, consider it the divine essence of a summer night, wrought in this perfumed marvel for themselves alone. They do not see me sowing patches diligently in spring, and they pass it in the daytime full of the exquisite scorn of ignorance.

There is one grievous eyesore this year due to the blistering heat of last, and that is the turf ; it is scarred irretrievably, in spite of liberal top-dressings and all the rains of winter ; it used to make a fine green carpet to carry the sundial and now it looks old and moth-eaten ; re-turfing is an expense I shudder to contemplate, but I suppose it will come to that when an infinity of labour and toil and fear and patience have proved that that is the only course.

I wonder if many gardens suffer as severely as the sandy gardens do in a hot summer. The lawns get to look like strewn straw, yellow and slippery with dryness. They are extravagantly top-dressed in autumn, but with all the care in the world there are always a rare lot of bare, dead patches. A good recipe for a spring (early March) top-dressing is to put four pounds of bone meal, four pounds of guano, half a gallon of soot, and half a gallon of lime to every barrow load of decent garden soil. This mixture well worked together, scattered liberally over the turf and then raked in, is excellent. It is wise to roll the lawns, during this treatment, after a shower of rain. I suppose the lucky people who have fine rich deep soil do not have to resort to these aids. I have often wondered what it must be like to have the garden of a friend in Northamptonshire, where " grass cannot help growing " ; lawns, while indispensable to any garden scheme, are a terrible trial on hot light soil.

The sundial looks well enough, despite its degenerate surroundings. In its grey solid respectable beauty it seems to repudiate the caprice of the surrounding turf, and claim admiration alone on the basis of its sober colour and comfortable proportions. The first sundial was of wood ; I had a nice old brass dial and tried to get a stone pedestal for it, but the price was always monotonously beyond my means, and so one day in despair we put up a section of tree-trunk, sank the dial into it at the correct angle (aided by a sailor-man guest) and tried to make it beautiful with ivy. It was never a success. One missed the fine grey stone colour and the decorative line that habit has associated with sundials in the mind's eye.

Then one day, long after, in passing a builder's yard, we spied an old terra-cotta chimney thrown carelessly in a corner, so old and weather-worn that its original yellow had long yielded to greeny-grey streaks on black-grey. We stopped, smitten instantly, simultaneously, with the same thought. " Don't see how we could make a top to carry the dial," I said doubtfully, but the sailor thought he knew, and we asked the price. It was 7/6 and was sent home that afternoon. I remember still how hot we got carrying it all over the garden and trying the effect of it from place to place.

At last we set it on the smaller lawn just out of reach of the shade of the apple tree ; here is a picture of it as it was then, hollow, base-less, and dial-less. When we had fixed its

THE GOLDFINCH ARCH IN BLOOM AND BOUNCER

HOLLOW: BASELESS: DIALLESS: THE CHIMNEY-POT BEING MADE INTO A SUN-DIAL

position we fetched barrow loads of sand,
washed clean by the brook in the valley, and
filled it to the brim, so that it stood firm as
solid stone. But somehow it needed a broader
base—it *looked* like a chimney pot, standing
up stark and straight out of the grass ; and
I did not want it to look like anything but a
rather ecclesiastical sundial pedestal. So we
found some broken bricks in the wood, and
those we mixed with coarse sandy cement.
After cutting an octagonal piece of turf away
from the chimney base we filled in with the
mixture. When it was nearly set we put a
smooth surface of fine cement all over, dis-
colouring it in places, working the corners
round as if worn by time, and lining out
the octagon in rays to look like separate
stones. It was a great success ; we laboured
on into the sunset, planning how to set the
dial in the top on the morrow.

Then we made our great mistake. We set
the dial, very correctly as to time, or rather
the sailor did, but we set it on a wooden block
which we cut to fit the top exactly. We laid
it on the sand and cemented it firmly in, **very**
finely, smoothly and carefully.

The sailor went back to his far wild waterways, and I watched the sundial telling the hours with all a creator's pride and pleasure. It was such a good piece of work, so nice in line and colour, that it was with a real pang I found it slowly splitting and cracking all round the top; it was always worse after rain. I asked everyone why it was, and no one knew; I was sure there had been a mistake but could not lay my hand on it. Two years later the sailor came back to find the historic sundial on the verge of dissolution, and its owner, after long suffering, reduced to philosophic despair. He knew the mischief at once and cursed himself roundly for a short-sighted fool. The block had been cut out of unseasoned wood, and the rain working through the screwholes on the brass dial had swelled the wood and split the stone. He was just in time to save it. We undid it, and took out the wood, bedding the dial this time in sheer cement; with a good deal of ingenuity, and a craftily cemented wire, we managed to heal the broken top, and now the sundial stands as the picture shows, in almost its pristine splendour.

I do not believe any finely carved stone piece would ever give me the pleasure that battered chimney does ; it has crept into the garden scheme with so much of happening that it has acquired its own traditions and stands secure in the affection of all on its own individuality. I believe that is the real way to make a garden—not perhaps a show place, but one's own beloved flower-shrine. I am aware that the chimney-pot is a deceitful imitation of the real thing, or that it might be called so very fairly, but to me it is no imitation like those " genuine antiques " of modern cast compo. It is the old terra-cotta chimney which we saw neglected in a builder's yard, it is the medium of many happy hours, and of some good toil ; it went into the Valley of Destruction for us and because of our ignorance, and we rescued it from there : it is not at all a chimney posing as a garden " piece," it is the dear old friend, rather sanctimonious and pig-headed, but still the nice sober old friend, who watches the hours by the apple tree, in bloom time and in fruit time, and who makes a good perch for the robins when they sing through their red throats in the pale winter noons.

If I were starting the garden again I would have the sundial set in a wide flagged circle with a rather formal design worked out round it in herbs ; creeping herbs like thyme and winter savoury should flow over the stone in designs, and a low hedge of hyssop or rosemary or lavender should surround it. It is pleasant to walk in the herb garden when tansy and tarragon are sprouting ; the pale green spikes are odorous ; the southernwood has a gawky look, its long lean brown arms each plumed tuftily with a grey-green feather. It has amusing names, " old man," and " lad's love." I like the pungent clean and acrid perfume of rue ; many people do not know that a few sprigs of it hung in a room will keep flies away. Also it has a charming way with gin ; a sprig put in a bottle gives this spirit a curious vague, almost pleasant taste. If people ask for an apéritif before dinner, and I give them that steeped gin with a dash of bitters and a thin hint of lemon-peel, they believe they have had a costly old-world cordial or a new American cocktail.

THE LOVERS HAVE LONG BEEN WED

THE FINISHED SUN-DIAL

Chervil is an annual herb, and may be sown for successive crops from the end of February to August; when about two inches high the leaves are ready for use. A sixpenny packet of seed will be enough for the whole summer. Tansy will grow anywhere; it is hardly worth buying, anyone will give a plant, and it will go on its way rejoicing directly it is set. Tarragon and southernwood like a dry, poor soil. Plants cost sixpence or ninepence apiece, and any nurseryman will supply them.

Rue likes shade, and a chalky soil for pre-ference. A good bush will cost anything from sixpence to a shilling. Rosemary and hyssop cost about the same, and like a dry light sandy soil. They both bear tiny purple blooms. Chives make a pretty border to a kitchen garden path. They should be planted in clumps (ninepence a clump is the usual price), and the tender spikes may be cut and cut; they always spring up again.

It's the housewifely soul of one that rejoices so much to see the herbs about their business; the flower borders are giving the eye exceeding pleasure, but the subdued and prudent joys of the herb garden are by no means to be

K

forgotten. Along the drills marked " Chervil"
now I see a thin green mist appearing, the
dandelion patch is full of form, and the tarragon will be ready to pinch when the chervil
is fit to gather.   There is no nicer salad than
one of crisp tender lettuce into which a
couple of chopped dandelion leaves have been
thrown, a tiny sprig or two of tarragon, and
a dozen little fern-like leaves of chervil. If
the cook uses chopped chives spikes instead
of the more aggressive spring onion, why,
nothing is left to ask for. The rosemary is
looking very robust ; it is one of the blessed
creatures which grows best in sandy soil,
so it has every opportunity of flourishing here.

It is good, too, to see the tansy and
thyme and mint so well advanced, because
that means I shall only have to buy ground
cloves for a fresh supply of moth destroyer.
If any reader revolts, as I do, at the smell of
the usual moth-destroyer (I do not know
what it is called, but you get it in white balls,
and put it among furs and blankets), she
would perhaps like to know how her house may
smell bearable, and yet be free from all fear
of moth. Take of dried rosemary and mint

half a pound each, of tansy and thyme four ounces each, of fresh ground cloves two table-spoonfuls. Mix these all well together and store in a well-closed box. If this powder is lavishly scattered among furs, blankets, and clothing as they are stored, no moth will go near them; the clothes moth lays her eggs in May.

Herbs which are cut and dried should be gathered while they are in flower, as at that time they possess the greatest strength. It is a good idea to hang them in a fair drying wind before storing. Rosemary stuffing for veal is excellent, we always use it; and many a homely cup of tea brewed from balm has allayed slight feverish attacks in the household! Balm is a nice quiet herb, a persistent grower and very shy in perfume, rather hinting at verbena than smelling a smell of its own.

Borage, which is alleged to make people brave, is a herb to use in " cups "; it grows violently from seed, needing less than no encouragement. Its misty blue flowers and grey velvet leaves are of great value where blots of cool colour are needed in the herbaceous borders. I remember well how, in my early youth, father came home with a young plant of borage, which was planted and tended with great care. Everyone was warned off it, everyone rejoiced when it came to bloom, and all admired the cunning black streak in its scheme of blue and grey. Next year it came up in larger quantities and thereat loud rejoicing. The third year father was discovered barrowing away a large quantity, " keeping it in bounds " he called it ; and the fourth year he openly alluded to it as a pest.

Some herb names are very quaint, " Poor man's pepper " and " staggerwort " ; " John-go-to-bed-at-noon " has a drunken sound about it.

Among the garden books I possess, and it is a motley crew, is one large heavy queer-looking volume called " The Historie of Plants by John Gerard, M.D., Physician to Queen Elizabeth, 1597, London." It is an enormously heavy book of 1,392 pages, with a complete index at the end. My copy is imperfect, the first 160 pages being missing, but there is enough in the rest to exercise wonder for years of reading ! After I have had an hour or two with Dr. Gerard I am filled with a sort

of terror at the difference between medical
knowledge of to-day and the medical knowledge of his time, a respect for his industry, and
a great amaze at his observation and knowledge. Evidently there were gardeners in the
land in those days.

He constantly refers to his garden ; he
always starts with a description of the plant
he is discussing in all its varieties, follows with
the places where it grows, then the time of
flowering, then the names in Greek and Latin,
and then with the most technical and intimate
discourse on the virtues of the plant. I
should imagine that all medicine in his day
was herbal. I have some favourites among
the plants he treats ; I like to read his dis-
sertations on the cresses. For instance,
reading thus of Indian cress it is slowly borne
in on one that he is talking of our old friend
nasturtium :

" Cresse of India hath many weake and
feeble branches, rising immediately from the
ground, dispersing themselves farre abroade.
The tender stalkes divide themselves into
sundrie branches, trailing likewise upon the
grounde, somewhat bunched or swollen up

at everie joint or knee, which are in colour of a light red, but the spaces between the joints are greene. The leaves are round, the footestalke of the leafe commeth forth on the backside almost in the middest of the leafe. The flowers are dispersed throughout the whole plant of colour yellowe, with a crossed starre overthwart the inside of a perfect purple colour. The seeds of this rare and faire plant came first from the Indies into Spaine and those hot regions, and from thence into Fraunce and Flaunders, from whence I have received seed that hath borne with me both flowers and seeds, especially those I received from my loving friend John Robbin of ' Paris.' "

One wonders what manner of man his loving friend John Robbin may have been. Someone who knew the old doctor's love of gardens, and troubled to send him, in those uncertain days of travel, seeds of a new and pretty " cress." He is very keen on the cresses, and proceeds to tell us that " Sciatica cresse hath many slender braunches, growing from a stalke of a cubite high, with small, long, and narrowe leaves, like those of garden cresses. The flowers

be very small, and yellow of colour, the seede
vessels be little flat chaffie husks, wherein
is the seede of a reddish golde colour, sharpe
and very bitter in taste."

I confess that I should not altogether like
to have a plaster of swine's grease and this
herb to cure sciatica if I ever had that unpleasant complaint.   I like the floundering
romance of medicine ; one gets an insight into
it from some of the prescriptions this industrious fellow sets forth :

" The   rootes gathered in autumne, saith
Dioscorides, do heate and burne, and are good
successe with swines grease made up in manner
of a plaister, and put upon such as are tor-
mented with the Sciatica : it is to lie on the
grieved place but fower howers at the most,
and then taken away, and the patient bathed
with warm water, and the place afterwards
annointed with oils and wooll laide on it."

There is something in the assured way he
tells of the virtues of the herbs which always
makes me long to go round and try them.
I am sure if I found simultaneously a plant
of his precious cress and a friend suffering
from sciatica I should make the plaster and

experiment on the "grieved place." His description of water-cress is really very charming. It smells of bread and butter and tea in country inns on hot summer afternoons :

"Water cresse hath many fat and weake hollowe braunches, trailing upon the gravell and earth where it groweth, taking holde and rooting in sundrie places as it creepeth ; by means whereof the plant spreadeth over a great compass of grounde. The upper face of the whole plant is of a browne colour, and greene under the leaves, which is a perfect marke to know the Phisicall kind from the others. The white flowers growe in spokie roundels. Water-cress being chopped and boiled in the broth of flesh, and eaten for daies togither at morning, noone and night doth cure young maidens of the greene sickness and sendeth into the face their accustomed lively colour."

I suppose, therefore, this is, though I never suspected it before, a cure for anæmia ; I like the name "greene sickness," and when one comes to think of it very pallid anæmic subjects have a greeny hue. I feel intimately familiar with his garden when I hear him talk of the way pyrethrum grows very plentifully there. He says, " It hath great and fat leaves like unto Fennel," which is true enough, though the similarity never occurred to me before he mentioned it ; I read, fascinated, that " Pyrethrum taken with honie, is good against all colde diseases of the brain. The roote chewed in the mouth, draweth foorth great store of rheume, slime, and filthie waterish humours, and easeth the paine of the teeth, especially if it be stamped with a little Staphisagria, and tied in a small bagge and put into the mouth, and there suffered to remaine a certaine space. If it be boiled in vinegar and kept warme in the mouth it hath the same effect. The oile wherein Pellitorie hath beene boiled, is good to annoint the bodie to procure sweating, and is excellent good to annoint any part that is brused and blacke, although the member be declining to mortification : it is good also for such as are stricken with the palsie."

The only useful purposes I, in my ignorance, know for pyrethrum are those I see advertised in 'buses, where, under the name of a

certain famous powder, we see the funeral of
beetles, and are told that it kills moths, fleas,
and every other harmful insect.

Nice old Dr. Gerard! There is a certain
border in my garden where grow scented
violets, very precious, very sweet, the dear
little romantic flowers. I fancy from the
amount of space he gives to them that he
must have been fond of them. He says they
have a privilege above others "not onely
bicause the minde conceiueth a certain
pleasure and recreation by smelling and
handling of these most odiferous flowers,
but also for that very many by these violets
receive ornament and comely grace : for there
be made of them Garlands for the heade,
nosegaies and posies, which are delightful to
looke on and pleasant to smell to, speaking
nothing of their appropriate vertues ; yea
Gardens themselves receive by these the
greatest ornament of all, chiefest beautie, and
most gallant grace ; and the recreation of the
minde which is taken hereby, cannot be but
verie good and honest : for they admonish and
stir up a man to that which is comely and
honest, for flowers through their beautie,

varietie of colour, and exquisite forme, do bring to a liberall and gentlemanly minde the remembraunce of honestie, comeliness, and all kindes of vertues. For it would be an unseemly and filthie thing, as a certaine wise man saith, for him that doth looke upon and handle faire and beautiful things, and who frequenteth and is conversant in faire and beautifull places, to have his minde not faire, but filthie and deformed."

He quotes a great deal from Virgil in connection with violets, and tells us how with the aid of them is made the colour of "yelloe Oker of Athens." Apparently he kept his eyes open for them in his ramblings, for he tells us how he found another sort growing wild "near unto Blackheath, by Greenwich at Eltham Park, with flowers of a bright reddish purple colour." It interests me because the most lovely variety in my garden, the one of which I have fewest plants and also, be it known, the sweetest scented, is a rather small violet of the same bright reddish purple colour! I suspect it is because he has a tenderness for these flowers that he finds such an ample list of their virtues in medicine.

" The flowers," he says, " are good for all inflammations especially of the sides and lungs, they take away the hoarseness of the chest, the ruggedness of the windpipe and jawes, tempereth the sharpness of choler, and taketh away thirst. The leaves of Violets inwardly taken do coole, moisten, and make the bodie soluble. Being outwardly applied, they mitigate all kindes of hot inflammations, both taken by themselves, and also applied with barley flower dried at the fire, after it hath lien soking in water."

He tells us how to make a syrup of violets and sugar, whereof "three or four ounces taken at one time purgeth choler." Here is the recipe ; I wonder sometimes if I were to make it and hand round three or four ounces at a time, when there is stress in the domestic atmosphere, whether peace would descend and anger turn to instantaneous smiles. Somehow it does not read like a very effective nerve sedative :

" First make of clarified sugar by boiling a simple sirupe, of a good consistence, or meane thickness, whereunto put the flowers cleane piked from all manner of filth, as also the white endes nipped away, a quantity according to the quantity of the sirupe to your owne discretion, wherein let them infuse or steepe fower and twenty howers, and set upon a few warme embers; then straine it, and put more violets into the same sirupe; thus do three or fower times, the oftener the better: then set them upon a gentle fire to simper, but no to boile in anywise; so have you it simply made of a most perfect purple colour, and of the smell of the flowers themselves. Some do add thereto a little of the juice of the flowers in the boiling, which make of it a better force and vertue. Likewise some do put a little quantitie of the juice of limons in the boiling, that doth greatly increase the beautie thereof, but nothing at all the vertue."

I love the quaint wording of that recipe. I have not yet had the energy to sample the value of it as a culinary effort. The virtues he ascribes to his syrup are astounding, as witness this engaging prescription:

" Sirupe of violets is good against the inflammation of the lungs and brest, against the pleurisie and cough, against fevers and

agues in young children, especially if you put
into an ounce of sirupe eight or nine drops
of oile of Vitrioll and mix it togither, and give
unto the childe a spoonefull at once.''

He has a potion which may appeal to many
readers : '' The leaves of mallowes are good
against the stinging of scorpions, bees, wasps
and such like, and if a man be first annointed
with the leaves stamped with a little oile he
shall not be stung at all.''

The only flaw I can find in this advice is
that it is hard to know when one is going to
be stung. He hints now and then at his own
opinion with a charming diffidence, especially
after he has offered a very shrewd opinion
as to the value and correct definition of some
herb. He tells us he is '' no graduate, but
a countrie scholler as the whole framing of
this historie doth well declare.'' I conceive
him a gentle soul, an ardent gardener, a keen
observer, magnificently intelligent. Sometimes in a lone hour I will read over and over
the following story. It is one of the parts of
the book which enable one to reconstruct the
times as well as the man. I like to bore back
into the centuries, feeling for the intelligence

of this human being whom I like, and struggling to achieve some contact with his
personality.

" I hope my good meaning will be well taken
considering I do my best, not doubting but
some of greater learning will perfect that
which I have begun according to my small
skill, especially the ice being broken unto him,
and the woods rough hewed to his handes.
Notwithstanding I thinke it goode to saie
thus much more in my owne defence : that
although there be manie wants and defects
in me, that were requisite to performe such
a worke ; yet may my long experience by
chaunce happen upon some one thing or
other that may do the learned good : considering what a notable experiment I learned of
one John Bennet a chirurgion of Maidstone
in Kent, as a man slenderly learned as myselfe
which he practiced upon a butchers boie of the
same towne, as himselfe reported unto me :
his practice was this : being desired to cure
the foresaide ladde of an ague, which griev-
ously vexe him, he promised him a medicine
and for want of one for the present (for a
shift as himself confessed unto me), he tooke

out of his garden three or four leaves of this plant Rhubarbe which myself had among other simples given him, which he stamped and strained with a draught of ale and gave it the ladde in the morning to drink, it wrought extremely downwarde and upwarde within one howre after, and never ceased until night. In the ende the strength of the boie overcame the force of the phisicke ; it gave over working, and the ladde lost his ague ; since which time he hath cured with the same medicine many of the like maladie, having ever great regarde unto the quantitie which was the cause of the violent working in the first cure by reason of which accident, that thing hath beene revealed unto posterotie, which heretofore was not so much as dreamed of. Whose blunt attempt, may set an edge upon some sharper wit, and greater judgment in the faculties of plants, to seeke farrther into their nature than any of the auncients have done : and none fitter than the learned phisitions of the Colledge of London ; where are many singularly well learned, and experienced in naturall things."

The poor lad,—who had only his ague-sapped resistance to set against the local practitioner's science !

One is divided between sympathy and mirth to hear him telling in the simplest manner possible of a potent purgative, which it seemed the fashion then to practice with. " This experiment was practiced by a worshipful gentlewoman Anne Wylbraham upon divers of her poore neighbours with good success ! "

To make young wenches fair and cherry-like he tells them to " take the roots of Monks Rubarbe, and red Madder, of eche halfe a pound ; Sena fower ounces ; annise seede and licorice, of eche two ounces ; Sea-viouse and agrimonie, of eche one handfull ; slice the rootes of the rubarbe, bruse the annise seede and licorice, breake the hearbes with your hands, and put them into a stone pot called a steane, with fower gallons of strong ale to steep or infuse the space of three daies ; and then drinke for three weeks togither at the least, though the longer you take it, so much the better ; providing in a readiness an other steane so prepared that you may have one under another, being always careful to keepe a good diet."

L

I can scarcely bring myself to imagine that these pungent herbs steeped in strong ale and drunk like water for " three weeks at the least " could make any maiden's complexion fair and cherry-like !

He tells us that the distilled waters of strawberries drunk with white wine is good against passion of the heart, reviving the spirits and making the heart merry. He tells us that wine is the sweeter by having water poured into it, and that those who in that manner drink it remain in health that before had their bodies feebled and over-weakened with pure and unmixed wine.

I am glad that the beginning of my garden library was Gerard's Herbal.

Books are wonderful things—and the books that matter, it seems to me, are those that convey a personality. "The Bettesworth book" does ; written by a garden lover about his gardener. I believe that such perfect literature, such poetic prose, such finely observed and nicely balanced portrait studies as are in that book and its sequel, "The Memoirs of a Surrey Labourer," have been written for posterity and a place among the classics

of this generation. It does sometimes happen
to one in one's life to be able to admire and
appreciate with the whole heart without
reserve, perfectly ; and I never cease to thank
Providence that it took it into its head to make
George Bourne and to let him loose on the
world in my own day ; for it is one of my
proudest privileges to know him personally.
Providence gave with a lavish hand to me in
this matter, for it set George Bourne and his
garden within a stone's throw of my garden,
and sometimes (rarely, because like all great
men he is a shy and distant soul), I go down
the lilac-grown garden path to his front door
and drag him from his books for an hour in
the garden " Bettesworth " tended.

There are some passages which take away
my breath for the simple and lovely way they
achieve their atmosphere.

". . . I ought to have been busy, yet I stood
and listened ; for the earth seemed busy too,
but in a softened way, managing its business
beautifully. The air seemed melting into
numberless liquid sounds. Quite near—not
three trees off—there was a nightingale non-
chalantly babbling ; from the neighbourhood

of the cottage came, penetrating, the bleating of a newly-born goat ; while in the orchard just before me Bettesworth stooped over a zinc pail, which, as he scrubbed it, gave out a low metallic note. Then there were three undertones or backgrounds of sound, that of the soft falling rain being one of them. Another, which diapered the rain-noise just as the young leaves showed their diaper-work against the clouds, was the all but unnoticed singing of larks, high up in the wet. Lastly, to give the final note of mellowness of flavoured richness to the morning, I could hear through the distance which globed and softened it a frequent 'Cuckoo, cuckoo.' The sound came and died away, as if the rain had dissolved it, and came again, and again was lost."

I never tire of reading this, and other passages like it ; it is a lovely thing for a craftsman to see his tools handled by a master-hand. Words are my tools, and I so fearfully hate the way I often use them that it is a real happiness to happen on such work as this.

CHAPTER VII

CATS

DOWN the grey stone path they come, one, two, three, four grey-blue pussy cats in single file. The evening wind stirs in their silken coats, the orange rays of sunset flash tawny sparks from their red-brown eyes. They walk daintily, grey silken pad after grey silken pad, with plume-like tails waving behind, and ears sensitively alive to every sound. I watch them with immense pleasure. They seldom walk together like this, and I can see how different they are, though so alike. Bluebeard's massive frame, low-built and cobby, so light and lithe of foot withal, is a perfect contrast to the mercurial Zillah, who is all fur and no frame—Zillah who leaps and darts like a fish in water, Zillah who is a prey to that most tyrannical heart disease, jealousy; and Madame

Mousie, wholly unlike them both with her aloofness and reserve, her huge owl eyes, and that fashionable patrician very snub nose!

Mimicking his elders in their stately progress, with his tongue in his cheek and a roguish grin, comes the kitten, last in the line, and threatening to break out of it with each impish step. He hates restraint with all his riotous little heart, but he cannot resist the fun of pretending he is grown up. He has a funny name, that little chap. The hot weather had made him very ill when he was quite tiny, and I grew so depressed about him that an unsympathetic paterfamilias advised me to " call spades trumps " and let him die. A listener, seeing I was by no means consoled, said, " Let's cut a pack, and if you cut old Mossy Face, he'll win the trick yet! " So we cut, and I miraculously cut the ace of spades. The baby puss was duly registered as " Old Mossy Face " in the great books of the cat fancy which are in Chancery Lane, and he never looked less like dying than the next morning when I took him his Brand's Essence.

It was the Bashi-Bazouk who first made me

really love cats. We lived in a flat in London then, and had no animals, until I came home one day to find cook had imported a lean, leggy, odd-eyed white kitten. I said he must go ; that cats were a nuisance in town, above all in flats ; that he was ugly ; that I hadn't asked for him, and all the rest of it. But I could not find a soul among all I knew who would take him ; they said they felt as I did, for which I could hardly blame them. Then I said he must be mercifully killed, and ordered chloroform to be used for his execution. As time went by and no chloroform appeared, and the white kitten, who by now had been christened the Bashi-Bazouk, began to develop a suicidal fondness for me, I perceived I must be strong and act myself. So I came in one afternoon with a bottle in my muff and qualms of disgust at the task before me, to find Bashi-Bazouk waiting on the mat. He followed me into the bedroom and jumped on the eider-down, purring a noisy welcome. He made himself into a round fat lump of whiteness, all hunched up and contented, with soft paws padding the quilt, and a blue eye and a yellow eye blinking at me in happy unison. I watched him miserably. I have never been very good at killing things. And then a mouse ran across the floor. I shall never forget the Bashi-Bazouk. From a foolish round double-chinned purring idiot he became in a flash a long sinewy line of muscle and movement, all hard purpose and determined rage ; so I hid the chloroform bottle, and told cook her kitten was too good a mouser to be killed.

He became so much one of the family that we never did a thing without consulting him, and his advice was always extraordinarily sound, except about the cottage. I took him on my knee one day—a massive lapful he had become, too—and asked him if we might look for a country cottage to spend the summer in, with a garden to grow asparagus for him, and sparrows for him to eat and trees to climb. But he was very upset. He begged me most pitifully to let him stay where he knew he was happy, and we nearly quarrelled over it. He said he knew every inch of carpet, every mouse cranny, every draught-proof chair. But the worst happened, for the cottage *was* found, and while I was busy distempering it I used to wonder how the Bashi-Bazouk would like the country. He had lived with us from kitten days in the top flat of a detached block of flats ; his only exercise had been on a lead roof. No one else in the building kept a cat, and he had never been known to go downstairs and out in the street in his life. So the upheaval for him was complete.

It took him a long time to learn things. The funny green carpet outside was a rare puzzle. It was green like the carpets in the flat had been, but it was softer in pile, and sometimes, especially in the early morning, it was wet. He would pad across it to and fro, immeasurably bewildered, cautiously shaking each paw at every step, stopping now and then to sniff at a daisy, and stiffening into acute alarm if a leaf were blown by the wind across his path.

Then the wood was an odd place ; it was full of the legs of impossibly tall chairs with shifty tops that shook and rattled. He found he was never scolded, however much he scratched those legs, and he used to come and tell us how he had never seen chairs before that had tempting twittering flying things in their tops. He found a laurel bush in due course, where he would sit and wonder, and try to get used to the noise of its leaves ; and never shall I forget the moonlight night when various neighbouring cats, having scented a newcomer from afar, came to visit him there and see if they liked him. He studied them with self-possession and amazement, frightened and curious, but courteous too, and then a hospitable instinct overcame all other emotions, and he led them to a dustbin and purred while they foraged for titbits. Such use to make of a summer night ! He learned better later on, and we used to hear his voice raised in an awful chant, and come across evidence of his popularity in the generations of white kittens which began to people the valley. When he died, full of years and honours, he was buried in rosemary and pansies under that selfsame laurel, and never, never could any of us bear to have a white cat to take his place.

A great many people are enormously cruel to their cats. They do not mean to be, but they are. They feed them irregularly, pet them spasmodically, and pay not the slightest attention in the world to their coats beyond stroking them now and again if they feel like it. Cheap cats are treated cheaply. It is a horrid thing to say, but it is true. No one pays a good price for a thoroughbred pet and then neglects it. I am pleading at the moment for the common cats, the haphazard little lovable wretches who infest our land, and are, in my opinion, a disgrace to it. (I would like every cat to be beautiful and beloved and cared for, but that, I fear, is a dream of Utopia.)

I was visiting the kindest-hearted couple in the world the other day, people who would weep to see an animal suffer if they knew it was suffering, and one day, in a stuffy outhouse on a sack, sweltering in the frightful heat, I found a lean cat with six young and ugly kittens—oh, beyond words ugly !

There was a saucer beside the little mother with dregs of sour milk in it, and her lips and nose were white with anæmia. It was the family mouser righteously fulfilling her destiny and reproducing her kind in the teeth of distressful neglect and indifference. It was only that they did not realise what they were doing. It was the greatest joy to regenerate their kindly hearts. When I left, pussy's lips were already faintly tinged with pink, owing to the generous diet which was putting new blood into her veins. The fuss and excitement over that little invalid! The excursions to the village to get fresh raw meat and cod's head; the saucers of green peas reserved from dinner for her by my anxious hostess; the painful task of removing mercifully five of the useless babies; the relief when it was over; the daily ceremonial of giving mother-puss half an iron pill. All these attentions altered the status of the forlorn little mouser, and when I heard last from my friends it appeared she had become fat and happy and beloved, with her own brush and comb, her hassock " de luxe," and her bran bath every Saturday to keep her coat clean and silky.

People say to me sometimes, " I don't know a good cat when I see it," and I invariably contradict them. They may not know a cat likely to win on the show bench when they see it among a lot of other healthy pretty cats, nor need they worry about that, for very few people do ; but they know a good cat. We all know one instinctively, I believe. A well-proportioned well-marked cat, in the pink of condition, with a nice coat and intelligent eye, is not to be mistaken ; and that is a good cat. I said " well-proportioned," so the ears will not be half the size of the head, the legs will not be lanky, the eyes not small and close together. Anything weedy is wrong and to be despised. An instinct for show points is a special dispensation of Providence, and given, I believe, to very few ; and when given, it does not always bring peace in its train.

With the demise of the Bashi-Bazouk came the longing for another cat, so one day the Master arrived with a tabby kitten in a fish basket. His company name we were told was St. Anthony, and he never sang at nights because of his name. We called him Tiddy-weeny for short, and he likes you best if you talk to him in a maudlin sentimental voice. He is a poacher and has a discriminating palate ; he worships the matters of the table. When asparagus and green peas are in season he superintends cook's movements with the extreme of fussiness, and after anxious hours spent running between the scullery and kitchen fire, he ushers the finished article into the dining-room with tense uplifted tail and devout eyes fixed on the dishes. It would be a trial none of us have yet dared to face to take either of these vegetables before his saucer is garnished and set aside to cool.

Tiddy-weeny was insulted once. It was in a hot summer when we all wanted to go to the sea. So we asked a friend to bring her maid from town and keep the cottage aired for us.

She was a bookworm and a spinster, and she had a heart of gold. I have said how Tiddy-weeny is a poacher—he eats a terrible number of young birds, and every spring he goes in peril of being vengefully slaughtered for the havoc he works in the wood. But somehow he gets spared. Anyway, it appears that he arrived home one night replete and satisfied after a sojourn far afield. He was gorged with young rabbit, and walked with discomfort, as greedy folk are apt to when they have done themselves too well.

Our friend spied him, and called her maid : " This cat is going to have kittens, and soon, too, I should think, by the look of her." So they set to work at once to make thoughtful preparations for Tiddy-weeny's babies. He was shut in the housemaid's pantry with a nice box lined with hay, and a lot of warm milk in case he felt thirsty or exhausted during the night. In the morning they opened the door gently to see how things were going on ; an outraged bachelor fled past them, and he never came near the house again while our friend was there. He had a lot to tell us when we came back ; as he said, " Chaff is chaff, and there you are ; but my character is my character and I value it." He was too angry even then to be very intelligent.

I think it was my friend's story of her preparation for baby-pussies which made me long very much, all of a sudden, to have some. And somebody said, " Why not do the thing properly and start with a thoroughbred cat ? "

I always like the best. So I blithely started from that remark into the thorny, tortuous, troublesome paths of cat-breeding proper. As I look back on this garden of mine and all it has led to I realise more and more strongly how good a title I have chosen for the history of it. Everything I have done in it and through it has been started in the blackest ignorance, and I am not sure that the learning has not been the loveliest part of achievement.

To return to the affair of kittens. I began to haunt cat shows in order to see what colour and kind of a lady cat I wanted, and at last there came a day when Tiddy-weeny found two fluffy blue-grey kittens being introduced to each other in the study. He was so unconscious of what they meant to his future position as lord of house and garden, that he was most pleasant, greeting them with fatuous good-nature. He patted their fluffy cheeks with his smooth brindled paw, looked into their orange eyes with friendly green ones, and wagged his tail for them to play with.

Madame Mousie, the beautiful aristocrat, was, as I say, introduced to Bluebeard, and formally betrothed to him ; but after a week's arduous flirtation thought better of it, and stoutly refused to look at poor Bluebeard, much less to enter into the bonds of holy matrimony with him. I built a cattery for them, and started them in life to the best of my modest means, but Mousie was extra-

TIDDY-WEENY

TIDDY-WEENY'S FRIEND AND FELLOW-POACHER

ordinarily obstinate, and I at last concluded she was an old maid at heart, and bought Bluebeard another wife. Now, although Mousie did not want him herself, she was extravagantly jealous of the new wife, abusing her in frightful Billingsgate, and making the welkin ring with her despair. So I let the happy couple have the cat-house to themselves and said Mousie might gang her ain gait. I regret to say the first use she made of her divorce was to give her hand to a low-bred troubadour from over the valley.

Within a day of each other the two ladies had families. Mousie came creeping round one day when Zillah was away from home and saw two lovely grey fluffy children on their warm cushion ; she looked at them very earnestly, while I watched her. Then she went off to look at her piebald mongrel on *its* warm cushion. There had been four of them, but we only left her one. She knew something was wrong ; she turned it over and over, then took it in her mouth and ran off with it quickly to the garden. When I reached her she was trying to bury it.

The Only-woman-in-the-world was playing

M

near by and ran up in time to see the rescue. She was immensely interested ; children do love gruesome things. I tried to explain in fitting terms that Mousie having made a mésalliance appeared to be ashamed of the fruits of it and to be doing away with the same.

The face-that-I-love-best-in-the-world turned on Mousie in tender pity, and then, intelligently wrinkling, back to me : " Then it's very important that Mousie should marry the right sort of husband." "Very," said I. . . . There was a long pause while this piece of new knowledge was digested, then :

" Mother, is it as important for grown-ups ? "

" More," I answered ; " because grown-ups are more important than cats."

It made me almost shiver in my soul's skin to see the little mind laying its hands on this great problem. Here was a girl-child glimpsing for the first time her life-work. By and by she said, " Then people ought not to marry for themselves, but for their children ? "

I was well content.

One of Zillah's pretty children being very heavy of bone I thought I would show him. He was christened Travellers Joy, and indeed the grey fluff on the hedges in autumn, which is sometimes called old man's beard, is very like the coat of a blue Persian kitten.

So one winter day the young man came up to town in a basket and spent a strenuous evening being bran-bathed. The next morning I took him to Westminster with a metal tally round his neck, tied with blue ribbon, in case he got lost, and put him in his pen.

Then I had a look round and decided Travellers Joy was a rotten specimen. I was convulsed with horror at my vanity and boldness in bringing Zillah's baby son into this august assembly. I hovered round the pen and nearly took him home, but he said he would prefer to see the thing through ; and I bolted like a coward and left him to it.

In the evening I returned to fetch him. He was most pleased to see me, purring and stretching, and smiling. There were three cards on his cage to show he had won a first prize, a second prize, and a special prize.

We went home softly, head in air.

The next day I took the dear little conceited creature on my knee and we had a long talk.

" Son of Zillah," I said, " you are very nice
and I love you, but your ears are too upright
and your nose is a little long. Shall I sell
you to someone who does not mind per-
petuating these faults, or will you take
monastic vows and be my little cat for ever ? "

He thought a very long time and then told
me all his heart. He said he had often dreamed
o' nights of becoming a troubadour in the
valley, of taking the romantic woodland
moonpath and wooing after his kind, to the
distress of humans, but that he had had a long
talk at Westminster with beautiful Blue-
jacket of Hyver, and that *he* had said grand
pussies, like they were, never roamed valleys
at will, but led a guarded existence in much
luxury, and were only wedded with great
pomp and much expense at the discretion
of humans. " And so, missus," he finished,
" I'll be your little monk, please, free to come
and go where I will through all the valley.
Marriage is stranger than fiction : platonics
will do for me."

I think he was right.   He is a happy person
now, free as air, loved with sacramental
fervour by the whole household because he

was our first pet to bring home prize cards. Singing is his hobby. Directly anyone touches him, indeed almost as soon as anyone looks at him, he bursts into loud rapturous purrs.

In course of time, when repentance had come to harvest in Mousie's bosom, she was royally espoused to that same great Blue-jacket of Hyver, and we wait on the tiptoe of hope for the princes and princesses to be born.

People are very funny about Persian cats. They think they are very delicate ; that they are selfish and undemonstrative ; that their coats are a dreadful nuisance ; and that they will die early from swallowing their long fur. I have not found any of these things. Persians, and indeed, I suspect, any cats, will succumb to pneumonia if housed in damp quarters. But dry shelter is not a great demand for any pet to make. I let my cats run free of wood and house and garden, unless they are being bred from, and a merry healthy happy lot they are. In the matter of fur, they are groomed every morning with a comb and stiff-bristled brush, so loose hairs stand little chance of being licked off and swallowed. That is a courtesy one extends as a matter of

course to all long-haired pets, so I do not see
there is any special trouble to be made about
it.

And as to their affection, no one who has
kept and cared for Persians will deny them
the warmest and loyalest of hearts. They
are more inclined to attach themselves—
dog-fashion—to one particular person and
to eschew strangers than common cats;
but that is a failing cat-lovers will readily
forgive. Persians are excellent mousers, very
keen and sporting. They are dainty in their
habits, clean, affectionate and extraordinarily
handsome.

People who have grown to like the neat
lines of a well-bred animal never lose their
taste for the best, and it is an excellent point
of view to encourage. I always believe the
sincere love of good stock, which is found more
strongly developed in Englishmen than any
other race, has helped to more of our national
success than is suspected. It means a tremendous lot, careful breeding. It means
patience and forethought; it means a very
great deal of trouble to direct such a strong
force as the mating instinct in animals into

a chosen channel ; it means endless watching, endless self-control, temper-control, nerve-control, control of greed of gain. It's a fine discipline.

Sex is a strange thing. Most people have a way of avoiding it, and of saying it is " coarse " if they do speak of it. But I think it is very interesting, and nothing in Nature is coarse if we touch it with clean hands. An ill-bred animal is the result of its owner's ignorance, which is the unforgive-able sin. Ignorance is the ugly child of laziness, which is selfishness. And here I am becoming dogmatic, which means I have become a bore.

CHAPTER VIII

LAWNS—THE AUTUMN GARDEN

I HAD a week-end guest once who told me the truth. She said " Good-bye. I like your cottage, but you ought to have something for people to do. Everyone is not mad on gardening like you, and everyone doesn't want to lie in a hammock and read. You should have croquet or tennis, or clock-golf."

I was very grateful for the hint at the time, and mused on the advantages of so honest a spirit in a guest ; but I have grown to hate it since, and see all the wisdom of a civilisation which says you should not criticise hospitality, but take what is given you and never come again if you are not satisfied. The trouble and worry that truthful woman has caused me ! First there was the performance of looking out a position for the lawn which must be made to provide the necessary entertainment, and when the gardener found it was to be taken out of the kitchen garden there was a dreadful uproar. He complained bitterly of the shortage which would ensue in peas and potatoes, and I could quite see his point.

A mistaken zeal, however, urged my case, and we finally marked out a good space of eighty-four feet by forty-five feet which lay sloping to the sun on the hilly garden. The levelling started in November, and took till the following May, as it very quickly proved to be a matter not of digging, but of excavation.

We had to pickaxe our way through rock sand to a depth of eight feet, and long before the level was reached and the steep banks sloped back to a good angle, I was heart and soul for the courtesies of life, with none of the bald honesty I had so applauded at first.

During the digging and barrowing (for cartloads of surplus sand had to be moved into a remote corner of the wood) a painful conviction grew in upon me that no turf, or lawn seed, was ever going to grow on that poor thin hot sandy soil. Here was a pretty dilemma !—one which has taken so much time, trouble, and thought to unravel that I am writing about it in case anyone is ever tempted to undertake a like labour.

The first thing was to give up all hope of a lawn for another year, and to spend the months from May to late autumn in enriching the soil in every possible way, in order that the turf might have a chance when at last it should be laid. The top spit had been carefully barrowed aside when the levelling began, and now was worked in with it rich imported loam, about half a cartload of the latter to a cartload of the former. The mixing was a herculean task, especially as the loam was stiff in texture, and had to be broken down first.

To each cartload of the mixed soil went two barrowloads of well-rotted farmyard manure, half a bushel of basic slag, and one bushel of lime. The rock sand at the deep end of the lawn was broken up a good six inches to act as a draining medium, and then the compost was spread over the lawn to a depth of ten inches, and left to settle

It looks kindly now, and as soon as a long enough spell of wet weather has set in to make turf cutting possible the turf will be brought in to be laid, and then I shall begin to see the end of the months of labour which five minutes of honesty caused.

The steep sides were a rare puzzle for a long time. I wanted to turf them, and plant them thickly with bulbs, but the toil of improving the soil on sheer slopes would have been immense and also very expensive. They were finally planted with periwinkle, St. John's wort, rock roses, and white broom. The roots of these plants will hold the banks up, and each in season will give charming bloom.

In time there will be hawthorn and laburnum trees round the lawn to shade the players and the grass from the full sun. Then, when the busy years have worked their share, the lawn will be a beautiful cool green shady place.

Enquiry showed that fifty plants of white broom would cost £2 10s., so I bought a shilling packet of seed from Carter and put it in the frame.

Weeks later a long day was spent in planting the sturdy seedlings, grown from that packet, in the banks. Each had a hole dug out deep and filled with good soil to give it a start, and there were close on two hundred! Patience is the gardener's gold-mine. Nearly two hundred white brooms for a shilling! These economies give me a mean close-fisted thrill, and make me long to be a nursery gardener myself.

Soils are curious tricky temperamental things. People who live among pines and heather seem to acquire in time an absorbing love of them, of them and all they mean, the harsh sandy soil, thin and poor, the spicy smell of resinous woods, the dry bracing airs that blow about them, the strenuous thrifty vegetation which alone can tolerate such neighbours.

Then, again, people who are used to pastoral country grow to love that : wide flat stretches of green river meadow, stately phalanx of oak and beech ; the deep cool fertile soil and luxuriant damp growth make anything else uncomfortable to the eye. And I have a couple of friends who are devoted to chalk.

Nothing has anything to say to them but chalk, so they have built a house on it, and are now making a garden to lead to the house. I was very interested to hear of this, and went officiously along to see if I could help lay paths or plant edgings ; but they proved to be the real thing and would have none of me. They liked me to be there and watch and talk, but I must not help at all. The " real thing " never wants help in her garden ; I mean casual outside help, such as I offered. She knows where every bulb is, she and her gardener. She has thought out every line, every corner. She is making her mistakes and learning by them, and happening on unexpected successes and learning by *them* every inch of the way ; any outsider who approaches with a trowel is an impertinence and a menace. The garden is the expression of her ideal, the wonderful unconscious piteously honest expression of herself.

I quite understood when I was turned down and put on a small muck-raking job, to keep me quiet. It interested me to watch these two fighting out their own fight with the local peculiarities of soil, and, incidentally, I learned a few things about what seems to grow on chalk.

I was astonished to see, for one thing, how luxuriant and strong were the wallflowers, these splendid allies of a garden, with their cheery green all through the winter, and their abundant perfumed blooms in spring. They flourished in that garden with a woody sturdiness which proclaimed beyond a doubt the suitability of their quarters.

And how the snapdragons grew ! They had massed a large bed of a very fine flame-coloured variety ; it was not the tall-growing plant, nor one of the dwarfs, but the in-between size, growing to about fifteen inches. The flowers were large and very brilliant, and the effect of the bed exceedingly fine, backed as it was by the young green of oncoming Michael-mas daisies.

They had all the usual colours of snap-dragons in other parts of the garden, and every cranny in the walls was splashed with their coral, pink, and rose.

The path devoted to "day and night smells" was a pleasing thing enough, for the mignonette and night-scented stock flourished there as

A BRICK-PATH

though they loved the limestone. I would watch the bees busy among the fragrant reseda-coloured bristles till day gave way to evening, when the starry blooms of the mat-thiola would uplift, and the pale night moths hover about them like flower-ghosts. A pretty path it was, of grey, irregular stones, on which the sober-coloured mignonette rioted like colossal moss. Just behind it grew a huge clump of love-in-a-mist, and, it may be fancy, but it seemed to me that in no other place had I seen that pretty annual grow so large or shine with so intense a blue.

My friends were very successful, too, with their phloxes, Canterbury bells, geraniums, and Michaelmas daisies, and when questioned earnestly about these flowers they said that as these plants all appeared to like what they found, they had not altered the soil for them, or in any degree gone out of their way to improve matters, except to see that the phloxes had plenty of water as they came into bloom.

They admitted that a certain fine young clematis Montana, which was already making great headway on the house, had been coaxed with a good heaped barrowload of fibrous loam, after the removal of a great deal of chalk, and that lilies had had to be humoured with peaty loam and leaf-soil. Gladioli, they said, were willing hearts, responding cheerily to a little fussing. It was when I found a very ill-tempered-looking rhododendron that I suffered my first pang of real sympathy for them. The situation had obviously been looked out carefully. There were evidences of great care in planting, as it was no stingy hole which had been dug out and refilled with good soil (of course I could only see its surface size—I do not know how deep they had gone). But that rhododendron was sulking, and I avoided looking at it whenever I passed its way.

Their greatest triumph was the dear little rose garden. To begin with, it was beautifully designed, coherent without being obvious (a rare combination), and then the roses looked so healthy. I have seen growths many times more luxuriant on kinder soil, but I knew— and every rose gardener knows—what interminable labour it means to get good results out of a shallow soil over chalk : the digging out and the filling in, the importation of loam and manure, the ceaseless mulching and watering and attention, the niceties of pruning in order to get the most without asking too much.

All these intricacies of rose-lore occurred to me as I sat among the fluttering petals of Madame Abel Chatenay, of Rayon d'Or, American Pillar, La Progres, Hugh Dickson, and the rest. I knew that the fairy scene my eyes approved, and heart could rest upon, had been achieved by months of earnest labour and by that loving desperate toil which is the hall-mark of the " real thing " in a garden.

Autumn is a welcome time in the tale of months. The comfort of damp cool misty morn and eve to round off the days, instead of the hard brilliance of July and August, comes to the senses with so much refreshment that one learns from it how really exhausting the heat of summer can be. In September, too, begins the joyous gardener's year— from early till late the trowel clinks its tune, barrows of loam and manure come trundling to famished beds, bone-meal and basic slag and sulphate of potash make a royal escort

N

wherever one goes, and the bulbs sit all over
the study in green paper bags, waiting their
hour, the plump meek creatures so brimful
of promise—and surprise. Mysteries they
are ! I sit sometimes beside them and take
them in my hand. Who would know, who
had not lived and learned it, that this shiny-
skinned small oniony-looking thing holds
a growing tulip, with all the panoply of its
leaf and equipment of its state ? Who could
see a clump of brilliant crocuses defying winter
and announcing spring in this small dented
corm, so light and pale ?

They were a great nuisance to me when I
began gardening four years ago. I thought
everything had roots like a daisy, and felt
bewildered and annoyed to hear of " bulbs."

In time I learned that a very large number
of the flowers I most gratefully admired grew
from bulbs. The daffodil, tulip, blue bells,
crocuses, lily, cyclamen, crown imperials,
some irises, snowdrops, and many others ;
also a bewildering succession of facts came
tumbling one over another on the heels of
this discovery.

I found that certain bulbs, crocuses,

cyclamen, etc., were called " corms "; that this difference in name did not really indicate much difference in habit, and that it was pedantic to insist upon it ; also I learned that bulbs must be planted at very different times ; a large number in the autumn, such as daffodils, crocuses, tulips, muscari, chionodoxa, snowdrops. Others, like certain varieties of gladioli and lilies, must be planted in the spring. I found some bulbs must be lifted after bloom time and wintered indoors. Some must on no account be disturbed having been given comfortable quarters in the first instance. I learned that always and invariably the leaves of a bulbous plant should be left to die down of themselves after the flower has bloomed ; to cut the green is to leave the bulb flowerless for next year. I learned which end up to plant them, and how deep.

I found there was a whole special science round bulbs, and, being lazy, hated to find it : I grudge finding a new thing to learn, because I know I shall have to set to and wrestle with it, and I do hate work. But I hate being done even more than I hate the labour of learning. And there you are. Between the two hatreds one has a lively time.

Every autumn I wonder which is more beautiful, spring or autumn. Just before spring there is a hush in the garden, a breathless momentous pause ; one feels, in the very blankness of the hedges and the smoothness of the earth, a rising life beneath, which is surging higher with every day, will soon overflow the bounds of winter and ripple to the farthest brim of the land. I love these grave intent hours in the happy valley, I love their speaking silence, their immeasurable meaning ; the autumn days when the flowers fall on sleep, soft silky days when the wet wind comes like sad kisses on a weeping face, the grim fighting hours of deep winter when frost is hammering at the lives of the flowers and earth withdraws all precious life to her fastnesses. I love them every one, but most I believe I love the hush before the dawn of spring. It makes me feel, myself, on tiptoe ; as though I too were about to come up to the light of day, the love of the sun, to the arms of the wind, and meet the kisses of the rain. Autumn colour, however, is very lovely.

Late in August the borders begin to look bright and cheery, with great bushes of Michaelmas daisies (asters) in every shade of mauve and purple, shafts of red-hot pokers, brilliant gladioli, and the many coloured dahlias. The places where the blue delphiniums held court in July are hidden by the taller growing asters, which have been planted for successional bloom, as I consider them one of the showiest and most grateful of autumn flowers, especially when one remembers that the colour-range runs from white through mauve, lilac, violet, lavender, blue, to rose and pink. I wot well that they are greedy neighbours in a border, with a grasping root habit and an extravagant method of growth, but it is perfectly possible to keep a stern eye on any rampant outbreak, and with constant division and attention to keep the clumps within bounds.

I have a great partiality for the aster amellus in its varieties ; it is a low-growing type of the Michaelmas daisy, very branching and floriferous. The blooms are large, the range of colour good, and varieties may be chosen to extend over a long bloom time. I find, too, that they are not so ravenous nor so encroaching as many of the other asters, and are better for cutting and house decoration. Of the aster amellus, Framfieldi and Marion are good varieties ; Grandiflorus is a good late bloomer, growing two feet high ; and of the Novi-Belgii, Arcturus is a nice blue, growing four feet, and blooming in September. But really the best way is to go to some nursery garden, or Kew, and see the different varieties in bloom. In that way one can make colour groups to suit the individual garden-palette, and learn the names by which to order them.

Michaelmas daisies (asters) grow best in deep cool fertile soil, but will " do " anywhere. They bloom long and grow strongly with the least attention ; even on thin chalky soil they will thrive, and W. P. Wright declares that though the chalk bank does not conduce to vigour of growth, it does to richness of colour. Very good clumps can be bought for 6d. each, and excellent ones of the commoner varieties for 3d. each from most nurserymen.

There is generally a good August show in the bed, where lilium auratum, red-hot pokers, and gladioli jostle each other. They are curious things, those last. I am never sure how I feel towards them; not warmly, I know, but respectfully, I think. They have no scent, they need staking, they are not hardy (generally speaking). So many disadvantages are hard to live down. Yet one would be very sorry to be without them, for they have distinction, they make fiery glades of colour, and they are good for cutting. The corms have a bitter enemy in the wireworm, which means that vaporite or apterite must be dug in before planting in soil where these pests abound. In clay soil they will not need watering, but in shallow a weekly libation of liquid manure will greatly assist the garden display if started when the buds begin to show, and continued through the flowering season. On rich and fertile borders the bloom spikes can be early cut for indoors, as the corms are safe to throw up others; they open so persistently up the long stem that they are a real boon to the housewife who loves colour in her rooms.

Gladioli are not hardy plants; the corms must be lifted in autumn, as soon as the leaves lose

their first green. Do not wait, as with tulips
and daffodils, till the foliage has died right
down. The sound corms should be stored in
a suitable place till spring. It is useful to know
that gladioli of the Colvillei, Childsii, and
Lemoinei varieties will stand the winter and
need not be lifted. At least, that is true in
my Surrey garden. I do not know that I
would like to lay it down as a general rule
for any soil or site.

Red-hot pokers are mostly late bloomers.
One plant made a horrid mistake last year,
and sent up a splendid spike in early June.
I shall never forget the astonished expression
of that lorn pioneer towering among the
columbines and Canterbury bells, nor the
obstinate courage with which it bloomed
stolidly from base to tip through weeks of
comment and criticism, and then descended
to the grave before it could tell that more
orderly generation of its kind pushing up to
the light of day what strange garden companions it had dwelled among. Mr. Compton
Mackenzie tells me one can have these plants
in bloom nearly all the year round if one knows
the special varieties, also that they range

from dead white to fiery scarlet; but I am only talking here of the ordinary autumn blooming orange variety.

Sometimes I dream of great groups of dahlias in every variety against the green background of imagined distant trees; little pompons, tight and prim, and flaunting cactus or pæony types. I can see them cunningly arranged to colour, white deepening to cream, cream to flame, flame to terra-cotta, and that again to dark purplish-brown. But the idea never materialises. I do not think it ever will—for memory is a strange mate.

Once on a time, long and long ago, when I was a little girl, I walked with father down a village street to call on a sick parishioner. We passed through her garden, and stayed a good while to look at some splendid dahlias. A day or two later we came again and found only a collection of blackened sticks. Father, who was a keen gardener, shook his head: " It was that frost the other night—winter is coming," and I can never see dahlias now, to this day, without a shiver of fear and dismay, for winter meant tortures of the direst to us children. We were brought up hardily.

Our chilblained hands would break the ice in the water-jugs, and our teeth chatter over our lesson books, through all that soul-searing time called winter. Dahlias sum up for me, in one blistering pang afresh every time I see them, the cold and pain and distressful discipline of our childish winters! It was probably an excellent thing for us if we only knew it.

Despite this I grow dahlias because I love the bushy busy way they have of spreading themselves out in the borders, and covering the patches left bare by earlier plants which are now over.

Then I like also the queer spiky blooms of the cactus varieties, and the untidy pæony-flowered dahlias; they are freer and less formal than the bright little tight little pompons. As moisture is the great need in dahlia cultivation, I find it essential to dig well and truly before I plant out the wintered stools in early May or late April, and while digging I see to it that a liberal dressing of well-decayed farmyard manure goes under the top spit. Then, even in a dry season, given hoeing, the tubers will thrive without continued watering.

My way of growing dahlias is the lazy way. Truth to tell, I do not care for them enough to go to the trouble of raising them from cuttings, from seed, or root division, though these are the ways to grow the finest blooms. Moreover, I only have a couple of cold frames ; all my gardening is done in the open, without artificial heat, so I am necessarily restricted in many directions, and put out my greatest efforts where inclination leads me. As there are three acres of ground, and only one gardener, whose chief devotions lie in the kitchen garden, it would be adding enormously to my labour to install glass. So the dahlias take their chance. Now and again I spend 4s. or 5s. in a few new varieties of good colour and habit ; every autumn the stools are taken up, shaken free of all soil, dried in the sun, and stored in a dry place till the following spring. For those who prefer it, it is quite possible to winter dahlias out of doors by heaping ashes over the stools in autumn.

Hollyhocks are not very popular nowadays, it seems. Yet there is a path in the kitchen garden edged on either side with sturdy plants, which looks exceedingly well. I tried the round rosette-like double varieties and disliked them, so took an infinity of time writing everywhere for single hollyhock plants in shades of cream, orange, and dark purple. No one had them, though everybody kept the formal ugly double ones. At last one honest firm advised me to grow my own plants from seed. And that is what I had to do. I have the greatest confidence in recommending the plan to others, for the single flowers are infinitely beautiful, and grouped in tawny and purple shades can disappoint no one.

The great golden-rayed lilies in the wood are invaluable in the scheme of an autumn garden. From early August they are a magnificent sight for weeks on, rearing their lofty spikes through the bracken and heather, and towering stately fragrant flowers over all the gorse and young rhododendrons. On one of my plants last year one spike alone had nineteen blooms—and from end to end of the garden one could glimpse the creamy gold of them through the trees. The partial

shade of their position suited them admirably ;
they were planted in spring in a glade open
to the sun but shaded with undergrowth of
bracken and heather, and now they will look
after themselves for years.

Some of my friends have asked me to
describe in this book how I make paths in this
garden of dreams-come-true, and with every
desire in the world to oblige everybody I
find myself totally unable to do this. I
believe it is a question of native wit. It
seems impossible to say in words how to lay
a tiled path. One gets the tiles, one stakes
out a path, one spends days or hours, as the
case may be, on hands and knees, and lo ! a
tiled path.

Pitched paths are a little more complicated,
but even these I have laid with no more
instruction than watching a local labourer
for five minutes in George Bourne's beautiful
garden on the hill. I saw that the man
hammered each stone beside its fellow the
long way down, so that only the small worn
narrowest surface showed, and then after
hammering a yard or so he swept sand across
the stones. It was obvious that patience,

a straight eye, and a little regard for the slope of drainage at the sides were all that was necessary to lay the stones. I have pitched the whole of the terrace since, and though the nobbly stones are not the most comfortable surface to walk on in thin slippers of an evening, the effect is undeniably picturesque.

The easiest paths of all, of course, to lay are flagged paths, because the stones are so big, the method is so obvious, and so large a surface is covered with each stone. I have secured a happy effect before now by using irregular York paving-stone, and pitching in the small interstices. Pitching-stones and paving-stones agree very well together, and where one is working round a design of rounded beds, as I was in this instance, the small pitching-stones are a more plastic medium to help keep the line of curves and circles.

Grass paths are very beautiful and very simple ; troublesome to keep in order with the clipping and mowing they entail, but very restful to the eye and feet. All paths are easy to lay in my garden, because I am working on sandy soil. If I had the clay for which my soul ceaselessly yearns in the interests of the

MAKING THE NEW WALL OF REINFORCED CEMENT

THE FIRST TERRACE "WALL" WAS OF WOODEN STAKES

beloved roses, doubtless there would have been a long tale to spin of the way to circumvent difficulties of drainage, and so on.

Cement is a nice thing to play with. When we first cut the terrace the wall was made of wooden sticks, through a strange short-sighted policy of economy, which in the course of three years rotted away, and then we set to work (having borrowed planks from the amiable carpenter in the valley) to make a new terrace wall of tremendous strength and thickness, of reinforced concrete. It was very simple, though the work involved was very hard ; every unfortunate week-end guest for weeks was pressed into the service, and left his dole of groans bedded in our terrace wall.

First we ordered several loads of rubble, a corresponding number of bags of cement, a couple of loads of scrap iron and washed sand from the bed of the brook in the valley. These ingredients were mixed with water into an intelligent slush and poured into the frame work of boards, barrow by barrow. The scrap iron was laid in while the mixture was wet, and thus the terrace wall, sixty feet long and four feet high, was built.

Four terra-cotta balls from the neighbouring local pottery and a set of rounded steps in the middle complete the most effective feature in the garden. The rough surface, as it originally stood, looked very well, but we found that the frost caused the cement mixture to flake off, so in the first spell of dry weather in the following spring the wall and the steps were faced with pure cement.

The first brick wall we built was a dismal failure, I well remember, because it fell down in about eight months. A kindly expert from a neighbouring cottage, who came prospecting at the noise of its fall, diagnosed the mistake we had made. He told us we put too much lime and not enough sand in the mortar. We started off again with the backing of his advice and made a successful job the second time.

Honestly, it seems to me that there is nothing one cannot do for oneself in the garden, if one is not afraid to go on hands and knees and slave like a navvy ; it wants muscle, and a certain amount of intelligence.

One of these days I am convinced I shall have a fountain ; I would have had it long ago if I had just known how to keep the supply system full, the main water being a precious and expensive luxury.

I like stones used decoratively, and I like to find in gardens that use stones with discretion, nicely clipped hedges. They are almost as bad as bulbs in the amount of knowledge they want and the special differences that appertain to them. Some want pruning severely in youth ; some want leaving alone.

The whitethorn hedge is one which wants the most severe pruning, I think, of any from its earliest infancy. Arbor vitæ and holly and yew, and also, I believe, box, should be left to run up quite a good bit before being topped ; and yet that piece of information is not wholly accurate, because now I come to think of it arbor vitæ should be trimmed both at the top and the sides, some time before the others, as otherwise it is likely to be straggly at the bottom. There is a good deal in knowing how to prune one's hedges. Laurel is best for autumn clipping,

O

and beech hedges in early autumn; white-thorn summer and autumn. Yew and holly, arbor vitæ and box are most successfully clipped in spring.

In suitable soils I have seen wonderful hedges of rhododendron, but those, of course, must be regarded as a luxury, indulged in by people who can afford the time and the space and money for them.

MAKING THE NEW TERRACE-WALL

THE FINISHED WALL

CHAPTER IX

GARDEN HOBBIES AND WEEK-END GUESTS

ONE day I was calling on a friend who kept me waiting; I took up the handiest book and began to read to while away the time, and lighted on a sort of treatise, a poetic handbook on the life of the bee by that modern journalist with a poetic flair, Maurice Maeterlinck. I found that a brilliant imagination with the power of expressing itself in exquisite language was here devoted to an obviously congenial subject. I was whirled away, spent and breathless, on the flight of daring fancy. There was courage in the work, courage and insight and philosophy, and an indescribable charm. The first page I read made me desire to look inside a beehive, a desire that had never overtaken me before, as I had always looked upon bees as dangerous little products, spiteful and capricious, whom it was some people's eccentric hobby to entertain. I well remember that first page I lighted upon. It was describing the inside of a hive as it would appear to us were we of the stature of bees. I suppose most people must feel as I did on first reading that book. It is well enough known now, of course, but at the time I happened on it it was not so universally read—and it came upon me with a thrilling strangeness. The romantic treatment charmed me completely out of myself, and I went straight from my friend's house to the nearest bookshop to get Maeterlinck's " Life of the Bee."

From the moment I read it the world was transformed for me into one flaming desire to get, and keep, bees. I devoured all possible practical literature on the subject, studied every form of hive and all modern bee appliances, worried to death with questions every expert I could find ; and at last, having set the whole household agog with interest in the new hobby, announced one morning that a colony of bees was coming from Welwyn that day, to arrive at the station by a certain train. We all went, in the sweet spring

weather, to meet the buzzing box, which by
this time, under the influence of Maeterlinck,
had become not a box of bees at all, but a
mystery palace where a wondrous queen
and indefatigable virgins and splendid lazy
knights of love were in transit to their home
with us. We had set the hive for their recep-
tion high on a slope of glowing broom, facing
the south sun, with a bird-bath close at hand
to supply them with water.

It was an electric moment when we opened
the travelling box and introduced them to
their new home.

Another electric moment came a week
later, when we opened the hive to see if all
was going well, and the bee-master (who had
come over to superintend this exciting
operation, and to teach us how to handle the
little creatures without fear of stinging) discovered queen cells, telling us there would
be no queen cells unless there was need of a
fresh queen. So we hunted through the
frames and found that that most important
lady had been damaged or lost in transit. The
work of the hive was considerably retarded
for a start by this misadventure, and our

knowledge of apiculture was very much enhanced, because we had the interest of watching the operations of hatching out a new queen. We found her at last one day, young and tremulous, newly born, welcomed with acclaim by her anxious subjects ; and we hovered round the busy hive at mid-day for the next two or three days to try and follow her miraculous mysterious nuptial flight. In due course our young stalwart first-born queen killed off the other newly-hatched rival queens, and with her empire entirely to herself commenced brood-laying.

All through the long hot summer we shared our happy flower garden with the merry bees. We grew to love them ; we learned to handle them fearlessly, and we studied them, faithfully following every direction of our friend the bee-master, who was as keen and fervent a student of Maeterlinck as we ourselves. After the heather harvest we gathered sixty pounds of splendid honey ; the hive was filled to overflowing with the populous joyous community. We fed them well, made them warm and cosy for the winter ; and then disaster fell upon our happy colony : some mysterious disease came and blotted out all our bees. I remember well the mourning and the tears with which we saw the jolly little creatures stricken, and the sincere grief with which we have missed them from the garden ever since. As Maeterlinck says : " They are the soul of the summer, the clock whose dial records the moments of plenty. . . To him who has known them and loved them, a summer where there are no bees becomes as sad and as empty as one without flowers or birds."

I waited, before starting with another colony, to try and learn something about this mysterious disease, but all I have learned of any real value is that it appears to be peculiarly and virulently infectious, so much so that with my next venture I shall use none of the old frames, hives, or feeding vessels— nothing, indeed, which I have used before. I believe if one starts with a fresh colony and absolutely new equipment there is a fair chance of doing well—an expensive but presumably ultimately economical method. My first original colony, which I bought from Welwyn, was extremely strong ; and I believe

that the whole source of disease lay in the fact
that I in my ignorance bought the rest of my
hives later on in the summer from a cottager
who had already lost three hives.

It is not everyone who has a garden that
has a wood ; ours has been one of the greatest
joys of the cottage. People with nice tidy
orderly minds come down for the week-end
to rest from the labours of town, and find
themselves invited to sleep out in hammocks
through the summer nights. They get wrested
from the ordinary routine of their days by
being taken for long rambles after dinner,
and forbidden to dress for that same meal.
Towards midnight, when most people are
making for the bedrooms in an orderly and
reputable manner, they discover strange shapes
flitting about clad in warm dressing-gowns,
with blankets thrown over their shoulders,
and it ultimately transpires that half the
household is bound for the wood, there to
spend the summer night in the hammocks.

I shall never forget the night I discovered
what it was like ; it was a hot night and I lay
in a hammock swinging idly, dreaming, and
watching the stars through the pines. Wrung

STRANGE SHAPES GO FLITTING TO THE HAMMOCKS AT BED-TIME

BREAKFAST AFTER SLEEPING OUT IN THE WOOD

by the force of habit I went indoors at last, and suddenly a fierce resentment of the stuffy bedroom, the low roof, and the restraint of a ceiling overcame me so much that I slipped on a warm covering, took a couple of blankets and a pillow, and went back to the wood to spend the night. There was all the great heaven to be had out of doors, and all possible protection in a devoted sheep-dog; so I lay under a canopy of pine trees stitched with blue, to watch the solemn progress of the night.

The soul seemed to travel a great distance on wings; I lay rested in every nerve. Far off a night jar croaked, and away down the valley someone went whistling " Ninon." I was laved in the incomparable stillness of the night; sleep fell upon me in great waves. When I awoke it was to a feeling of something piercingly sweet. A fair breeze blew, the lungs were filled with aromatic air; away in the lane beyond a nightingale was trilling his song to the dawn. It is in the May moon that the nightingale sings best, and away down the valley others answered him, some so far that the only note to reach my ear was that long low whistle, the rarest and the sweetest and the best one to carry of all the notes of a nightingale. The famous jug-jug, which is always referred to as the characteristic note, is to my mind an ordinary hum-drum and very domestic sound. (I can often distinguish that low sweet whistle in the day time through all the songs of the other birds, while the much over-rated jug-jug is completely lost in the general clamour.)

The red light on the pine trunks grew warmer and fuller ; it came creeping through like a great smile. Unmindful to miss any of this glad hour I got up and walked the rose-garden, while the singing birds rose one by one and made their music to the dawn. By and by a lark started singing in rivalry to the nightingale, and I listened to the two, comparing them. The nightingale, for all its romantic reputation as a bird of song, has none of the rapture, the gathering ecstasy of the lark ; and again, the trill of the nightingale is ineffective compared with the trill of his rival ; at least, that is what I felt when I heard the two together.

For an hour I walked among the roses,

partaking of the busy beautiful life all round.
I watched the pigeons rousing ; I saw the
cats go slinking home ; I learned the intimate
early morning life of my pets as never
before. All the dawns of all the former
years had gone to the heavy drugged slumber
of indoor air and beds. I walked the garden
like a god, filled with the fresh lightness of
the morning. Beside me ambled my adorable
protector, with loving eyes glancing through
his heavy fringe, like deep brown pools
through reeds. When the bird-chorus lulled
a little in the press of domestic commissariat
duties, I went back to my hammock and
slept again profoundly, till the breakfast-
hour found me brimful of enthusiasm of the
newly discovered joy.

I believe more people would keep sheep-
dogs if they knew what wonderful guards
they are. Bred in the very marrow of them
seems to be a protective instinct. They
make no fuss about it, they do not go round
yapping and boasting about their job ; but
they are always on the alert to guard the
homestead of a night, and they seem to know
without telling when to come on duty. For

instance, when I take my dog Bouncer for an evening walk with friends he frolics all over the place and enjoys himself in his desultory fashion ; but if I bid good-bye to my friends and turn to walk back alone he comes to my side without a word, and walks, as long as I remain alone, with his muzzle to my knee.

He has a fair wife hidden away in the valley ; she is the working sheep-dog of a farmer, and their puppies always have, straight away from the beginning, a perfect instinct for following. We put the little creatures, tailless and fluffy like toy bears, on the ground, and they stagger behind one's heels, following each foot in turn till the eye grows dizzy to watch them.

Sheep-dogs are capable of the most perfect training ; they are highly nervous sensitive and particularly picturesque animals. People who really love them seem to love them to the exclusion of every other variety. There is a certain enthusiast on the breed, Mr. Aubrey Hopwood, who wrote a most fascinating book called " The Old English Sheep-Dog " ; unfortunately it is now out of print, and the only copy I ever possessed I borrowed from Mrs. Oakman (the owner of that celebrated champion Shepton Laddie), in order that I might quote some of it here, as his descriptions beat anything I could attempt to compass. " In character," he says, " the bobtail is an animal of quite exceptional charm. Of his sagacity there can be no question, and any specimen of the breed, tactfully handled in his youth, can be trained to accomplish wonders as a drover's dog, for the instinct of the race is ineradicable. Further, he can be trained with little trouble as a first class retriever."

Mr. Hopwood goes on to describe his ideal sheep-dog ; the colour scheme he advocates is " blue and white, the former predominating. A blaze of pure white lies on skull and muzzle, chest and fore-paws, but the remainder of head and body is of so wondrous a tint of blue that Nature seems to have overlaid her work with a thin veneer of hoar-frost in the moonlight . . . The breadth of skull and limb, the heavy, shaggy coat, the spring of ribs, the stoutness of loin, and the massive muscular quarters, all detract from any suspicion of legginess or length of back. Despite his inches, he has a peculiarly cobby and active appearance . . . Lead him out upon the grass, unhook his chain, and let him go loose. He gallops like a racehorse, hind legs well under him—active and lithe beyond suspicion, and fast enough to head the wildest Welsh sheep that ever led revolt upon his native mountains. He moves like a trained American pacer, the fore and hind leg on either side of him working simultaneously, with a quaintly indescribable waddle— a long stride which waggles the whole hindquarter from loin to toe at every step."

When I first came in contact with this delightful book I applied the rule of its precepts to Bouncer, whose pedigree proclaimed him of the best blood. To my inexperienced eye he appeared to fulfil every requirement of the most exacting judge. I enrolled myself therefore a member of the Old English Sheep-Dog Club and proceeded to exhibit master Bouncer at the next Club show. Mrs. Oakman, the owner of the aforesaid illustrious champion, helped me to "dress" him for the event. Bouncer was tubbed, taken into an empty room with a lot of straw, brushed and cleaned with chalk until he groaned with self-esteem. He was then put in a taxi and taken to Aldridge's by his breathless owner, where he faced the judges with amiable good humour and came out with two " very highly commendeds " instead of the first prize my fancy had painted for him. When I looked from him to Shepton Laddie I plainly perceived his inferiority. Coming that day, as I did, in contact with all the finest examples of a breed I sincerely admire, I was filled with a burning desire not only to own, but to breed, for myself, the finest possible example ; and then fate worked one of her rare wonders. A little man with a shrewd and kindly face, whom I knew to be Mr. Birch, the owner of the famous bobtail bitch Champion Home Farm Britannia, walked round the benches studying the exhibits. He glanced at Bouncer and was passing by, when I asked him in a humble voice how his Britannia was. He stopped and looked at me, and then looked again at Bouncer.

" Yes," I said, " he has a heart of gold,

but he is no good for show. I wish I could breed a first-class sheep-dog for myself and then show it; there would be some satisfaction in that." Then Mr. Birch said, "Why don't you buy Britannia?"

I laughed, because a hundred guineas, which I was sure would be the least he would ask for such a famous and beautiful bitch, was not lying ready to spend at a moment's notice in a homely purse. I told him so, and we had a long conversation. The little man was kindness itself to me. I shall never understand why he finally sold me Britannia for a sum I could afford, when there must have been plenty of people who would have paid the full price and been glad to get her. I think he was very fond of her and wanted to be sure of getting her a good home when he gave up keeping sheep-dogs; or I sometimes even suspect him of a sporting desire to give the beginner a leg-up. Anyway, Champion Home Farm Britannia changed hands a few weeks later. The Master brought her home one day, almost sulky in his masculine effort to hide his pride in her beauty and the record of her wins.

There was a melancholy episode when her nuptials became imminent. A marriage was arranged between her and Champion Shepton Laddie. A lady of such high degree must wed royally, and that was a fact that poor Bouncer failed utterly to take into consideration. He cried himself hoarse outside her kennel, was seized with a virulent attack of love, and utterly refused to eat, carrying all his bones and biscuits to lay at the lady's feet, spending every moment of the day serenading her, and describing the condition of his heart. Early one morning, however, she was ravished from his gaze and taken to town, where she espoused the aforesaid monarch of his kind, and returned to tell Bouncer that she was a lawful wedded wife, and another's. An immense feeling of responsibility pervaded the household on the day she presented us with five puppies. Time is yet to show if my dream is to be realised and I have bred a winner.

For anyone who wishes to breed or possess dogs of exceptional excellence, the only way to gauge the quality of stock is to exhibit from time to time and measure the points

P

of the dogs against those of other owners and breeders.

There is a great deal written and talked about the corruption of the show ring, but I think average intelligence will reassure one that favouritism, if it is practised at all, must be only in very minor degrees, because after all the judge is judging under the fierce light of the public eye, and any flagrant divergence from the standard of points laid down for his guidance would attract strong and immediate attention. Besides that, human nature is a very good thing ; human nature is not really a cheat. People who love dogs really love them, and the man who is judging the particular breed of dog to which he devotes his attention and time and money must be obliged, by his enthusiasm, to give the prize to the dog that evokes his sincerest admiration.

People have said to me before now, " So and so is judging to-day, and therefore Such and such will win," and when I have had the curiosity to ask why, it has nearly always transpired that So and so knew Such and such very well, and had handled

WHERE THE WINNING SWEET-PEAS GROW

A BOB-TAIL PUP AT TEN WEEKS

his dogs frequently. It occurs to me, without any ill-feeling in the matter at all, that it is very possible that when a judge finds himself confronted with several excellent specimens and is hesitating as to which he shall award the prize, the fact that he has handled the dog of Such and such frequently, and knows to a hair's breadth its quality, may lead him to award his judgment to his friend merely because his superior chances of knowing the animal gave it just that much advantage over the rest in the ring; and upon my soul, I can see no cheating in that.

I have been sometimes asked if there is profit in breeding bobtails. I have not been in the fancy long enough to say very definitely, although I do know that I recovered half of the original price of my champion bitch in the sale of her first litter, reserving two of the pups to rear and show myself. If either of these prove to be a first class dog I shall be disposed to say sheep-dogs are very profitable indeed. I asked Mrs. Oakman one day what hers had cost her, when she had only kept sheep-dogs two years; she said that it cost her £200 up till then, and a few days later her husband told me that she had refused £500 for her champion to an American at a show. She has refused more since.

There is something sporting, I think, in taking an animal one has bred oneself, whose parentage, upbringing, condition, and appearance are the outcome of faithful thought and attention, and passing it under the scrutiny of the eye of an acknowledged expert to be judged with other people's carefully bred idea of *their* best, in taking one's beating with a good heart, in learning where one has failed in breeding to type, and in starting off again to correct and improve with the ultimate hope of winning.

At last I have got honesty to grow. For a long time it seemed that it would not grow in my garden, and I did not like the idea at all. Seedlings vanished like the dew; I believe they were zealously removed as weeds.

In a far corner of the kitchen garden grows a Maiden's Blush, a rose common enough, undisciplined in habit and growth, untidy, even parochial. A prolific rose, so lavish of bloom that it has never had the grace of rarity, never been a show rose ; indeed, it is generally labelled " out of date " nowadays, and only found in old-fashioned gardens like this. It is, for all that, so exquisite in colour, so sweetly scented and so unassuming that I love the bush and use the petals extensively for pot pourri.

Down along the valley is another garden, and the first spring I saw it it was a bewildering haze of pale blue forget-me-nots, among which grew some fine warm purple flowers. I admired the colour scheme, and found the purple flower was honesty, so I set forth to grow honesty too. But it took years ; I had to wade through sloughs of bitter experience to discover how capricious and how coy is honesty. It flowers like a weed where it pleases to grow, and refuses to be coaxed into growing anywhere that it dislikes ; it is a most cranky and temperamental plant. Judge then of my pleasure when one summer, in the fullness of years, I found a plant growing of its own accord, as sturdily as any plantain, in my garden : it had chosen a shady patch of ground under the Maiden's Blush.

The very next season I found there was growing alongside of it a hefty bush of rue. Under the Maiden's Blush first honesty, then rue. I have long grown to know my garden has a humorous soul and is a crabbed friend full of quips and cranks ; but when it starts off trying to pose as a moralist and a prig I interfere. I hate sermons, even in flowers. So I hunted up another rose called Maids of the Village, and planted " lad's love " alongside, and these I watched good and hearty, that neither honesty nor rue should have a look in at that little romance.

There is no honesty in love, or, if it comes, then follows rue. My garden was quite right. What is the soul that moves in a garden ? It is the same soul which makes stinging-nettles grow furtively and secretly among forget-me-nots. I am always weeding them out. I suppose it is the same principle in a garden which in people makes them indulge in that fearful mysterious exercise—thinking, that ceaseless frightful submerged liveliness within us which is wholly divergent, try as we may, from that which we show our fellows in our words. We fumble with words,

trying to model with them images of our
thoughts. Goodness knows why we do. It
is a futile exercise ; speech is but broken
light on the depths of the unspoken.

Talking of honesty in love reminds me of
the dear lovers who have trodden the rose-
path in this cottage of dreams-come-true.
Hospitality is a curious thing; there are
times when I feel as if the house were full of
children, children adorably grown and intelligent, who take all one gives in the most
lovely faith, with no question or complaint ;
children dependent on one's thoughtfulness
for comfort and content. They come from
town jaded a little, tired of the swift current
of days rushing through the pent City cañons
of brick and mortar ; they spread the precious
week-end hours wide to the sun, the flower-
lands, the fluent airs ; and sometimes in the
still peace of moonlit woodlands lucky ones
have happed upon the glamour, the illusion,
the divine dishonesty of love ! Lucky lovers.
Easy guests to entertain. They want no
more than to be left alone, and for that they
give a boundless gratitude.

They make tears easy, somehow, in their

happiness. Perhaps I suffer from an abnormal sensitiveness to the pathos of things. It is a great nuisance, because it gives a distinct sensation of pain, besides laying one open to the reproach of being maudlin. I get the painful tears in my heart every time I remember some things. One is the sight of a *very* little boy walking beside a coster's barrow late one bitter winter night. He was exerting himself greatly to keep up with the stride of the man pushing it. The tiny lungs laboured bravely, the fat legs straddled, one hand was held up as if to grasp some other helping hand that was not there. A street lamp flashed the picture indelibly on to the films of my memory. It was evidently the end of a busy day; the barrow was fairly empty, the man was going home, in a hurry to get out of the cold. As they receded from me I heard him growl, "*Come* along, yer lazy 'ound," and saw the lazy hound making a superhuman effort to get some extra pace out of his little fat legs. I longed indescribably to pick him up and tramp with him beside the barrow "piggy-back," only the courage was not great enough. Funny little boy!

I can't imagine why I feel so pained to think of him. I believe it is because he was not crying.

Another memory is that of an old gentleman who was poor and something of a cripple and loved flowers. I gave him a new choice clematis once. Some months later I was calling, and when I caught sight of him, said, " Well, how goes Venus Victrix ? " His daughter answered, in the tone of accumulated grievance one hears in families where small events assume enormous proportions, "Killed! He *would* mess about with his beastly fertilisers." The old man scuttled off instantly like a blackbeetle who sees a light. A mental picture struck instant pain into my heart : I saw the dear old creature fussing over the new plant, unable to leave it to the processes of time and kindly offices of the earth, trying to accelerate and encourage strong growth with some of his artificial manures, and suffering a daily martyrdom at the hands of his exasperated family when providence saw fit to blast his efforts with failure. I was incredibly sad for him. And I felt so sorry he went away ! As though it

mattered ! He might have had a new clematis
every week to kill, if it occupied his thoughts,
and if only he would not be frightened of me.
But I couldn't tell him what I was feeling,
or do more than say, "What a pity!" to his
daughter, because of the shyness which looms
like a great cloud over human things. So he
never got another.

And another thing I can never forget is
the tragic brown eyes of a half-witted village
boy who loved to go orchard-robbing when
my brothers were home for their holidays.
He would slink after them exactly like a dog
that expects to be sent home when detected
following. He hid behind trees, and stalked
them, always with infinite cunning, laugh-
ing when their pockets were successfully
filled. But once he was impelled to declare himself. The boys, spoiled with success, rejected even the sweet warm apples
the birds had chosen to peck (always the
sweetest on the tree), and were presently
startled considerably to see a look of profound
reproach turned up to them among the
branches. "They little beaks be quite clean,
master!"

I started talking of week-end guests, and somehow wandered away to orchard-robbing.

As our garden began to demand more and more labour from us so did our point of view of friends change! We began to look on every friend with new eyes of critical appraisement, weighing up muscle and calculating the will to work. Dominated ourselves by a savage energy we shot it into their veins too, forced it in, like air into rubber tyres, and surrounded ourselves at the week-ends with an aura of demoniacal energy, goodwill, and perspiration. The change in tempers was extraordinary; some who came down peevish with self-esteem went back mild as milk, gentle and humble after a heart-to-heart fray with spade and wheelbarrow. It was exceedingly interesting to see them change like the Chinese paper flowers one puts into water, and unfold from stiff straight-laced stems into all manner of supple and astounding shapes.

Amusing episodes sometimes occurred over friends who, in town, were loud in their demand for exercise. One night at a dinner party the Master found himself taken to

task by a learned doctor who is also a
poet.

" You want exercise, my man ! Good
honest wholesome exercise. I never get
enough of it. You can't in London, and if
you go to the country it's all done for you,
what with motors, and beaters, and aero-
planes and all ! "

We listened in grave accord. When the
croquet lawn was in process of being hewed
out I set myself to plan a party of guests
who had complained of want of exercise in
London. There are always plenty to choose
from. I remembered the poet-doctor ; a
soldier-man who is also a playwright, and who
told us whenever we saw him that he loved a
spade better than his pen ; then there was
a singer who spends unwilling days in the
City earning the leisure to sing ; and (by way
of leaven) a little writer I knew, a clever and
very pretty writer-woman with red hair and
little hands and a desperate love of gardening.
A very eligible collection for helping with the
croquet lawn, it seemed to me.

The Master brought them proudly down
one Friday evening by the dinner train, and

handed them over to the sheep-dogs and me at the station with an appraising glance as if he would say, " Very nice raw material for the lawn." After dinner the singer gave us of his best, aided by the tiny hands of the writer-girl, who suddenly shone forth as a sympathetic accompanist. With the seasoned intuition of a hostess I realised that to-morrow would find two missing from the excavations below the wood. The poet-doctor became very depressed when we told him he was at last within reach of good honest wholesome exercise, but the warrior was full of joy ; he told us how to make a secret storehouse for food in case of invasion, and asked which of the animals would be eaten first when that gave out.

He was a broken reed. After an hour with the pickaxe the next morning he adjourned to the inn in the valley to " buy cigarettes," and there he made himself extremely popular, first frightening the honest rustics with tales of imminent invasion, then rigging them up a target in a sand-pit to practise their shooting, and finally treating everyone to old ale. I am bound to say we all left lawn-digging in

the end, except the doctor, and took rifles
and revolvers to the sand-pit, where we had a
joyous campaign and introduced the soldier-
playwright to the " Spotted Cow swizzle "
—an insidious apéritif which those who
have once tried always try again.

The doctor was a marvel. He worked
incessantly, very greatly to our surprise,
because his air on arrival had been anything
but content. Now that the lawn is levelled,
turfed, and played upon he reminds us
occasionally and without wrath of the lonely
work he did. The lovers have long been
wed, and often refer with shameless glee
to their first introduction to an " exercise
party."

Most of our friends have had a hand in some
part or another of the garden labours—reluc-
tantly or joyously ; almost every inch of
ground can yield its queer tale of merry
bungling and glad endeavour.

MIS-USE OF THE WEEK-END GUEST

THE DOCTOR WORKED ON ALONE

CHAPTER X

HOW extraordinary a child's imagination is ! When I was little we had a garden which was to me a place of mysterious sweet scents, a paradise of forbidden fruits, a dreamland of splendid colour. After we left the house and I grew up, that garden remained big and spacious in my memory. I longed to see it again, and renew for a moment the brimming hours of childhood. There was a flower in it whose name I did not know. Father brought it home one evening in a pot, and planted it amid the silent scrutiny of several pairs of curious eyes. We asked its name. He told us, but it was a grand name, difficult to pronounce, so we never laid hold of it. In due course buds came on the plant, and at last they burst into large purple flowers, which gave me so intense a joy that I would suffer a physical pang of sheer pleasure in their beauty every time my glance lit upon them. For several summers my young eyes watched that plant bear its wonderful blossoms, and in later years I would lie of nights guessing at what it could have been, and fitting to it all the nicest flower names I had ever heard: asphodel, and Venus' looking-glass, and passion-flower, and lotus. In dreams I saw the purple petals yielding to the breeze, and felt again the reverent ecstasy which had possessed my little body years before.

Chance took me the way of that old house not so long ago. I found a wizened dwelling-place with a mean strip of ground beyond—the palace, the paradise of dreams. In memory had been such beauty, in reality was such a shock. My fairy flower was a clematis, and I left the place marvelling at the happy simplicity of childhood. I wonder what magic dreams engulf the little women of this generation, as they lie abed listening to the wind singing through the trees outside their windows, what memories their environment is storing up for their later years, and

if they will ever revisit their homes to learn
the littleness of facts, the boundlessness of
dreams !

Do we remember often enough, we grown-
ups, how ardent are the small souls growing
up alongside ours in the awful fateful progress of the years ?   Do we pause often enough
to remember that the influence of ourselves
upon them now is what we have to answer
for at the bar of posterity, that as we yield
our children to the race so we shall be judged ?

The longer I live the more surely do I understand that it is the children who matter,
and that the saddest thing on earth is a barren
woman ; whether of choice or necessity, there
is nothing sadder or lonelier.   If good matters
at all, then children are of supreme importance, because they embody the good in this
generation, being guided to better in the next.
Looking back on time one feels very strongly
that that is the trend.   Stumblingly, with
many backslidings, but still surely and persistently, human nature attempts to improve
in the coming generation what it has deplored
or suffered in the last, and more than ever I
believe women at least, if not men, begin to

Q

understand that it is not the having of children that is wrong, but the having of unfit children, whether legitimate or not, ill-equipped to render a good account to the community.

If I might be a law-maker I would apportion capital punishment, not to the taker of life, but to the giver of life who gives it knowing it to be tainted at the source.

Queer little adorable things children are! To hold a fat slug in long clothes, blinking and yawning, is to hold the thread of eternity, the thin thread from " was " to " will be " which binds the universe.

Girl-children are brought up to believe that money falls on them by some benign plan of providence through the hands of men, fathers, brothers, husbands, whatever they may be, but men they are taught it is, who exude money and to whom they must turn when they want a trifle of their own to spend. An outrageous system! When my woman-child grew of an age to like pennies the whole falseness of the way we teach girls to get money burst upon me. I remembered how I had looked for money from anyone but myself.

I wanted my woman-child to feel the sacredness of money, never to be afraid of it, to look at it fearlessly as a powerful friend who can be called to aid always by the magic wand of work. I wanted her to feel clean and brave about money, because I remembered how I had always been ashamed of its very name, because I never had any. I had not been, as I should have been, decently ashamed of myself for not knowing the way to get it, but I was always anxious to hush up any reference to it as a disgraceful skeleton in the cupboard, as something nice people could not refer to. When I had any by a chance miracle I would spend it foolishly, extravagantly, heedlessly, because I had no idea of what it cost to earn, and indeed my whole attitude to that big vital problem of civilised life was vague in the extreme. When the Only-woman-in-the-world some years back came a-begging for a penny I was thrillingly conscious that now I must face for her the thing that had terrified me all my life, and that if she was to find comfort and not terror in money the task to teach her was at hand ; so I said, " You can have a penny when you have earned it. That is the only way to get pennies." What was earning ? she asked, and learned without dismay (because words have so little sense in baby ears) that earning involved work. We left our dolls that morning, I remember, and helped Nanny shine the silver, for which we earned two pennies and spent them as we thought fit.

In a year or so came the inevitable moment when a kind relation offered a shilling, but my joy was great to see that already the habit of working for money was settled, and that the little creature hesitated to take it, making this astounding remark, " But I haven't worked for it yet." The petrified old lady was about to press the rejected coin, around which (because she had never earned a whole shilling yet) a pair of large eyes were beginning to revolve with intelligent hope, but I intervened, and later on, when the buttons were sewn on great-aunt's gloves and her packing had been " helped," the shilling changed hands.

And so the seed was sown and tended, till now there is a sturdy plant of independence growing in the girl-child's heart which it is my constant joy to see. It sounds quaint enough at times ! The querulous youth in the seaside hotel last summer, who sulked all the afternoon when his mother would not give him the money for the " sweets and bait " he was always crying for, got small sympathy from the young woman when he told her his troubles. " Why don't you earn it, then you won't have to ask anyone to give it you ? "

Presently she will have to face an idea that has never troubled her yet, and that is, that however willing one may be to work, there is not always a job to find. And so by degrees she shall learn how skilled labour is really the only labour to take to the world's great mart with any surety of wage, and when she has chosen and mastered her craft, whatever it may be, I shall feel at last that I have met and killed for her the Apollyon of my own upbringing.

The Only-woman-in-the-world is nine now; she was five when she first had her garden— that is to say, she had an untidy slip of spare ground in a shady remote corner given to her to play about in, as is generally the lot of children, but that should hardly be called a garden. At first she planted mignonette and nasturtiums and candytuft and mustard-and-cress zealously enough, labouring with her tiny tools in that forbidding site, while we grown-ups looked on indulgently and laughed, and thought no more, as is the wont of grown-ups. She used to water her little bare feet regularly for a time, and was elated when crowded seedlings jostled up to the light, fighting for air and space. She neglected them entirely when bloom time came, and her patch gave her only a straggling bloom or two here and there where was a lustier plant than the rest. She spent her time instead in the big garden, where care and trouble had made fine borders and long gussets of colour. As my garden grew more and more to me, I resented seeing hers neglected, and asked her one day why she did not work in it still. She said, " It doesn't grow like yours does : it knows I'm little." It flashed across me that it never would grow like mine did for all the coaxing in life ; also that if her strip were in my hands I should leave it to the bracken and never try to grow anything in it. And then the injustice of the whole thing gave me pause. Why do people give the little ones

the useless sour strip of ground to learn their
first gardening in ? Why do they discourage
them from the lovely life of flower-tending
by giving them a soil and site they would not
be bothered to try themselves?

I looked down to the earnest face of the
woman who could not make her garden grow
because the flowers " knew she was little "
and so took advantage of her.   I looked down
and learned in a blistering second how selfish
and how cruel it all was.   The little hands
had tried, and the little heart had hoped,
and there you are. We had smiled indulgently,
knowing her labour useless, and been superior
and clever, we grown-ups.

So the woman and I gave ourselves a treat
that night. We sat up to watch the moon
steal like a dainty sickle between the pines—
a great treat, because she was seldom up
to see the stars and moon, those early days
of her life. We swung in a hammock late
into the summer evening while she designed
her garden. " I would like a gate and an
arch and a lawn and beds like yours, and I
should like it all to myself with a hedge,
so I can shut myself in and have tea-parties."

The arch must have a Lady Gay on it, and there must be a rose tree in the very middle of the garden. When she had gone to her bath, tired and excited and full of moon-and-garden talk, I drew out a plan of her garden as she wanted it to be. There was a good deal to be included in it, but I meant to have all she wanted, so I planned a big circle to be planted with privet for an outer hedge, and under the hedge four beds with grass paths between, then more grass, and a circular bed in the middle of her " lawn " to put the desired rose into. A little rustic gate was lying, I knew, in the outhouse, which would make a pretty entrance, and a wire arch to support the Lady Gay would be easy to buy.

We went out together quite early next morning, and found a large piece of ground sloping gently to the south. On it we drew a very big circle with a piece of cord tied on a stake. Then we dug that out. To this day I remember the labour of cutting turf under a blazing sun, and the round, fat face under its sunbonnet beaming with interest. She was very exigent. There was no resting to be allowed. We had to cut out the whole design in one day. It grew and grew exactly as it was planned, that garden. A final

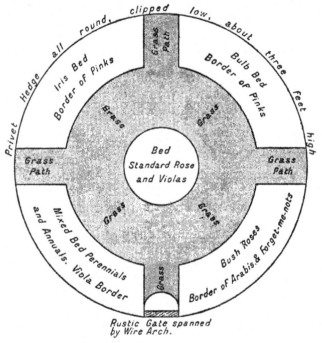

PLAN OF "MUFFET'S" GARDEN.

touch of inspiration came when we cut down the wire arch so that it made a low one about four feet high, just right for the little gate and tiny privet hedge. Grown-ups have to bend to go into Muffet's garden. Now that

time has helped us the low arch is a very
beautiful sight indeed. It has a Mrs. Flight
on one side, a mass of pink bloom in June,
and a Lady Gay the other, which repeats
the lovely colour in late July. The hedge
is comely and well clipped, the beds fully
stocked, and the soil with constant working
is getting to be of a very decent kindly
nature. I explained to her, when she wanted
to plant things wholesale in a hurry, how thin
and poor her soil was, and how hungry her
flowers would be. So she learned the pleasing
properties of manure and the staying qualities
of loam. It pleased me to find the potential
mother in her was shocked at the notion of
starving her young plants. She required,
indeed, so many " forkfuls " of manure that
we gave her a little wheelbarrow ("laid"
next spring by a miraculous Easter hen in
an enormous egg in the wood), and a plaguey
mess she makes of herself giving the seedlings
and roses " plenty to eat."

The Madame Abel Chatenay rose in the
middle of the garden had the extreme of
attention. She took four months to make the
bed for it. With slow labour, digging out and

digging out, small spadefuls at a time, wheeling away the yellow sand in the little barrow, at last she was lost to view in a vasty hole four feet deep and three in circumference. Then came the further labour of filling in. The hole was soundly besprinkled with basic slag for a beginning, and then lined with rotted turfs filched from a treasure heap in a lone corner where I had fondly hoped it was forgotten by all but me.   It was delightful to find those sharp bright eyes had spotted my miserly trick and knew the purpose and value of the hoard.   I laughed for joy of the dishonest little human I had borne, for sympathy of the many journeys which must have been made, trundling a tiny barrow in front of a throbbing heart.   I knew, well and well I knew, how my baby girl was shadowing forth all mother-love in the trouble she was taking to house and feed the coming rose bush.   And I knew, because I was always myself an extremely naughty child, what exquisite delight there was in diddling the elders and carrying a daring robbery to a successful finish.   So, stricken with convenient blindness I avoided the gaping pit in Muffet's garden till I saw good progress had been made in filling it with a rich and luscious compound of loam, leaf-mould, manure, bone-meal, and basic slag.

When the bed was full to overflowing we wrote the important letter to the nursery garden, ordering a standard Madame Abel Chatenay. After some weeks, during which the heaped soil subsided and settled till what had been a round bed with a humped middle became a round bed with a middle scooped out like a saucer, there arrived the carefully packed and long desired rose bush. She took it away to plant. I did not interfere in that supreme hour, but leaned on the little gate, and watched her spread the roots out carefully in a " nest " of warm sifted leaf-mould, watched her put the guardian stake alongside, fill in the hole, and then " tread in " with busy little feet. Year after year the blooms on that bush surpass any in the whole garden, hers or mine, for depth of colour and size of bloom ; year after year she reaps her lovely roses, babbling sanctimonious precepts, the adorable little prig. " It pays to do a thing properly in the first instance," and " Pity you have not planted all your roses as well as I planted mine," and so forth and so on, delivered at short range by a maiden to her mother—a truly modern picture.

One of the greatest successes has been the border of pinks. I well recall the extravagant day when we walked over to the local nursery and bought four dozen strong young plants of " Her Majesty," for Muffet's garden. Searching enquiry told the little woman that some of the nice old manure in the wood mixed with loam and leaf mould would make a handsome enrichment for the border they were to edge. So strenuous hours followed with a spade and wheelbarrow, and at the end of the day I found a grimy happy tired little soul planting the last of the pinks into a border bursting with good things. We sat on the grass and talked about the pinks for a long time—how they had had a nasty shock, truly, in being lifted from their first home and carried over long roads in hot hands, with newspaper round them ; but that now they would be extremely foolish if they did not quickly learn how well we meant by them in their new home. (They have rewarded her gallantly, I may say, and she is very proud of that border.)

It is a great joy to me now, as well as to her, that miniature garden, set on a sunny slope right in the middle of the big grown-up garden. It is a sparkling gem, brimful of sweetness and of colour, the garden of little Heart o' Gold, where she watches the round of the seasons and grows gentle and patient tending her flowers.

.   .   .   .   .

Gardening leads to strange thoughts. It leads me to feel sometimes that prayer is collaboration. I " pray " when I am planting things carefully ; that is to say, I collaborate to the best of my knowledge with nature, which is my idea of prayer, hoping for the best, having done my best; she and I, partners, lovers (adorable, difficult, incomprehensible, savage and strong, I love her), working together wrench beauty from the barren spots of earth. I pray like every other mortal body, stumblingly ; for prayer is feeling in the dark.

I feel when I read old Gerard's Herbal that he, directing his keen intelligence

into the darkness of ignorance about him,
trying to light on his steps and those of his
fellows a little way along the path of knowledge, was praying gloriously with the whole
of himself every time he found a new plant
or suspected a new use in it for the good of
man ; praying in every word he wrote in that
astounding Herbal of his. And there with that
word goes my religion, religion gathered from
the garden I have made and loved.   Collaboration is the great goal for which we all
aim ; every politician who thinks out some
scheme whereby the small efforts of the many
may bring some colossal result for the general
good is a priest at the great high altar.

Every self-wish slain, every human impulse
making for comradeship and general understanding and collaboration in the communal
life, is a step to the real religion.   Collaboration is much less vain than individual effort.
Marriage should become collaboration, family
life collaboration ; the worship of God, whatever and wherever He is, a great simultaneous
onward striving to collaborate with Him.
The State should be a vast collaboration of all
its units.

I look forward to the day when women are in the heart of the State instead of in the lap of it as they are now, to the day of divine collaboration when every woman, setting her son with his feet to his life work, will say, " Grace go with you, my son. I have done my part, the best of me is yours—a fine strong untainted body. The State has educated and now needs you. It is for you to prove how well we both have done our part."

Gardening, too, leads to some strange diversions. One of my most derided joys is to spend the winter evenings studying catalogues. Conscious of seeming lunacy, I go away into corners to have fits of enthusiasm alone, and emerge hours later flushed and excited, dishevelled, having wallowed in imagined loveliness till the brain reels. Catalogues have the most magic siren music in their pages ; they wile the money out of purses. I always believe that the thing conveyed to my imagination by the written word will bloom ; it never does, because my imagination is like an electric torch and touches everything with an unearthly light. But still, industriously,

indefatigably I go on hoping, and all the while
the earthly is good enough for me.   I never
want anything better than the western light
on the roses in June, the flat tender pensive
light of lost daylight and coming night ;
it runs into the nerves like embalming fluid
into the veins.

The catalogues make me picture wildest
loveliest confusion of colour, and they end
by bringing me up against the loveliest
accidents.   I write down enormous lists of
what I should like to get, lists far beyond my
purse to realise, and much larger than the
little garden could ever hold.   Then ensue
torturing days of rigid self-discipline.   I cut
down item by item and whittle away the list,
arguing each one painfully out of existence,
descending into abyssmal depths of despair
and argument as the list grows smaller and
smaller ; then there is generally a revolt of
nerve and temper, and I emerge back from
this secret civil war into the family life a
jaded wreck, with a list still infinitely too
big, but considerably reduced.

It frequently waits at this stage for a
fortnight or so, and then renewed battle,

R

generally this time in consultation with enthusiastic members of the household, who bring the light of their fresh intelligence to bear on the matter, and reduce things to a more or less reasonable proportion.

I come out of the imagined garden as I have lived in it with the help of catalogues, and face reality as if it were a strange land. The garden as it exists to the alien material eye is not in the least my garden as it exists to me. There it is, a strange mysterious fairyland of ever shifting shapes of beauty and glades of miraculous colour. If I were a futurist painter I could paint the most marvellous picture of this garden of glad endeavour as I see it with my two eyes, the mental eye and the physical eye; and after all, I believe that is the end of the whole matter—whatever gives scope for imagination gives happiness.

So the garden becomes, like Bottom the Weaver to Titania, a peg to hang dreams upon. Only, unlike the graceless weaver—insensate unappreciative clod that he was—the garden snuffs up the incense of work and love as would a god, regally extending

CHAOS IN THE ORIGINAL GARDEN

GROWING INTO SHAPE

the hand to kiss, flashing a dazzling smile of pure beauty to urge us constantly to further finer effort.

Sometimes I feel it is rare presumption on my part to have written this book at all ; only I feel so sure (with the hardihood of years) that many fellow-humans must start a country cottage in nearly as vile a state of ignorance as I—and I want to write to them, for them, in language devoid of knowledge yet tinged with understanding, while my ignorance is hot upon me, before I have arrived in the groove of routine where technical terms are everyday talk, those technical terms whereby the beginner is utterly bemused, and terrified into the stupid coma of humility, those technical terms which bespatter almost every garden book I have ever read, and the lack of which here will cause all serious minds to turn in loathing from this my tract.

APPENDIX

HERE is the end of the book. And looking it over I am appalled to see how exceedingly useless it is. As a rude but honest relation said, " Give it some guts, girl, give it some guts." I assimilated the advice with excellent grace because the title he gave me was pleasing, but the question of guts was very puzzling. I have now decided the best and most *solid* thing to do after all this frothy chatter is to enumerate every flower I have mentioned, with some idea of its habit and best environment. Gardeners will like it and never find it dull, and readers who are not gardeners can call this chapter an appendix or a catalogue and skip it with ease because it comes all together at the very end of the book.

Pansies will grow in most soils ; they love moisture and good loam, so that if the soil they are to go into is thin and hot, it is as well to enrich it with cow manure. If pansies are to thrive—as they will—in full sun they must have a cool rooting medium. They respond readily to generous treatment, such as an occasional watering with liquid manure, and if long-continued bloom is desired it is essential that every dead bloom be removed before seed pods form. Pansies may be grown from seed planted without heat in March (to bloom in July if well treated). Some of the best to mass in colour beds and borders are Bronze Kintore, deep copper; Countess of Kintore, purple and white; Mrs. E. A. Cade, yellow (a very sweet pansy that smells like honey and blooms very early in February); Seagull, white; Archie Grant, blue; Duncan, mauve, and, of course, the lovely Souvenir of my long quest, if it is in the market now.

Tree Lupin (Lupinus Arboreus Lutens) can be had in lilac, white, or sulphur yellow. It is deliciously fragrant and grows year after year, five feet high to a fine evergreen tree like a standard rose bush, if properly pruned.

Irises.—The ordinary rhizomatous irises (Germanica) will grow in almost any soil;

they are the well-known " flag " irises. The
Florentine, the white flag iris, is a beautiful
and free flowering variety. The rosy lilac
May Queen, the blue Princess Beatrice
(Dalmatica), are also very charming. The
rhizomes should be barely covered with soil,
and increase very rapidly once they are established. The yellow flag iris, a soft creamy
sulphur yellow, is a very beautiful variety.

The Dwarf Bearded Crimean Irises will
grow almost anywhere, even on old walls, I
believe, though I have never tried them there.
They make lovely edgings to the herbaceous
border, or fine groups in the rock garden.
They should be planted in early autumn,
though they may be moved as late as April.
I am inclined to the belief that a rather dry
and sunny situation is best for them. They
dislike fresh stable manure and should be
planted shallow like their grown-up cousins,
covering the rhizomes or root stalks only
lightly with soil.

Unguicularis (Stylosa) should be planted
in the autumn in a warm dry situation,
sheltered from the morning sun on light rich
loam. It is an abundant bloomer.

Alata, the beautiful scorpion iris, thrives best planted in rich light soil with a dressing of old manure. It is a lovely winter blooming iris in varying shades of blue.

Spanish and English Irises are bulbous and thrive readily in very good light soil, whether in the open or partial shade. The earlier the planting after the beginning of September the greater the success. Some fine varieties in the Spanish (June flowering) are : The Thunderbolt iris, and California, a good yellow to mass with it ; the Moore, golden brown and bronze shade claret ; King of the Whites, a new fine white large variety.

Of the English irises which bloom in late June and on into July : Clara Butt, a lavender-grey flaked with lilac ; Blanche Fleur, a rosy white ; Perle des Jardins, pale china blue ; Rosa Bonheur, white splashed with dark carmine. The English irises are very much larger than the Spanish and give a magnificent display.

Rhododendrons I have dealt with already pretty thoroughly.

Pinks may be propagated from cuttings in the autumn, and thrive in most soils, with a little help. The best varieties are Mrs. Simkins, Her Majesty, and Ernest Ladhams.

Lupins, Forget-me-nots, Foxgloves, Wall-flowers, Hollyhocks, Sweet Williams, Canterbury Bells, Snapdragons, Columbines sown at flowering time and pricked out when big enough into nursery beds, and later when they are bushy plants transplanted to borders where they are meant to bloom, will give hundreds of blooms the following year.

Broom may be grown from seed, but that entails patience. Most people buy plants and save the waiting time. They may be planted out at any time from pots. If grown from seed, the white variety is best put in a cold frame and planted out at the end of May to bloom the following year. Brooms go on increasing from year to year in size and height.

Tulips are a family by themselves, and deserve reams of writing. They will make, in their infinite variety, a brilliant garden display from early April to the end of May. Any ordinary garden soil enriched with old stable manure, with a sprinkling of quick-lime dug in while fresh, suits tulips. They should be planted from October to November, not earlier, and about four inches deep. Here is a small list of good garden varieties :

Duc van Thol.—Scarlet, dwarf, very early.

Pottebakker Yellow.—A clear large yellow flower.

Thomas Moore.—Improved. A lovely deep orange-flame.

Cottage Maid blooms after Duc van Thol, and before Thomas Moore. It is a rose tulip flushed white.

Wouverman.—A fine deep claret-purple. It beds well with Princess Marianne, a white tulip.

Couronne d'Or.—A handsome orange double flower.

Gesneriana Major.—A fine late tulip for bedding and distant effects. It is a full crimson-scarlet, with a blue-black centre. It is a tall grower, reaching as much as twenty-four inches.

Didieri Alba.—A pretty creamy white, fragrant, height about fifteen inches. It is a late blooming cottage variety.

Feu Ardent.—A medium-blooming cottage May flowering tulip of a dark glossy crimson, very glowing and insistent in the garden scheme.

Duchess of Westminster is a fine new Darwin late-blooming tulip ; flowers very large and globular, of a bright salmon-rose. The Duchess grows twenty-eight inches high.

Fine mixed Darwin tulips produce a grand effect when grouped in the herbaceous border.

Sweet-Peas are flowers I have strenuously avoided mentioning throughout the book, inasmuch as your sweet-pea lover is as narrow-minded an enthusiast as your rose lover. I have no doubt that if my soil were rich, or if I had two or three gardeners and an unlimited purse, I would be a sweet-pea enthusiast ; but seeing that these lovely flowers are gross feeders and need quite as much attention as the rose garden I have left them severely alone, being unable, from some innate contrariness, to tackle them without a distant hope of doing them justice. Books have been written about sweet-peas ; every garden paper has its columns devoted to the subject, and anything I may try to say is an impertinence. Seeing these flowers even boast a society of their own, the National Sweet Pea Society, it is plainly obvious that they need no words of mine to urge their claims.

Heleniums are handsome plants for the herbaceous borders, like small sunflowers; they will grow in any soil and should be planted in autumn. They increase rapidly into large clumps as do Michaelmas daisies.

Montbretias grow very well in any ordinary flower border enriched with manure, but prefer a sunny situation. Plant out from November to March and cover early plantings lightly with litter.

Montbretia Tragedie.—The very dark purple and orange montbretia, growing three feet high.

Prometheus.—A large montbretia of a brilliant fiery orange; a very vigorous grower and very expensive at present.

Montbretia Crocosmaeflora, carrying large spikes of red and golden flowers to a height of two and a half feet.

Stocks, like night-scented stocks, should be sown in patches for successional bloom during March and April. "All-the-year-round" is a splendid little wallflower-leafed stock, forming compact bushes ten inches high and blooming snowy white. A succession of bloom in the early flowering sorts is maintained best by sowing at intervals from early March to the end of May.

Crimson Gem is a valuable new dwarf bedding ten-week stock.

The Brompton Stock should be sown in June or July to bloom the following summer. Seedlings should be wintered on a dry border or in a cold airy frame, to be planted out in the spring.

Lobelia is generally planted out, with the bedding stuff in July, from boxes containing a large assortment of well-grown plants on the very verge of bloom. It is an easy way of filling the beds (if a lazy and expensive way) to buy boxes of seedlings of all sorts of summer herbaceous stuff, like tobacco plant, stocks, asters, snapdragons, etc., from the nursery gardener, and plant them out in their season. For people who have not many frames, or space or skill to raise their own seedlings (by far the cheapest and most interesting way), this plan may be commended.

Roses have been fairly thoroughly dealt with in the chapter devoted to them, but I append a list of varieties other than those mentioned. Every nursery gardener stocks roses.

Prince de Bulgarie.—A strong-growing amber-pink rose, inclined to be uncertain in colour.

Lyon.—One of the loveliest of modern roses. A shrimp-pink in colour. Very heavy in the head, too heavy for its stalk, and I have never seen it growing consistently yet. It always has a straggly bush, mildews easily, and has a low trick of withholding its glorious colours when it is in the sulks.

Mrs. John Laing always annoys me, because with all her virtues she manages to convey an impression of vulgarity. She is a florid hearty pink, brimful of scent, carries herself magnificently on long strong stalks, blooms through a very long season, and is a good-natured easy-going handsome piece of goods.

Betty.—I love Betty. She is one of the warm rose-copper coloured Hybrid Teas; growing sturdily into late autumn, with great graceful flowers and beautiful red-bronze foliage.

Mrs. Wakefield Christie-Miller is a rose I have not yet tried, but mean to, because

Murrell says of her that she is "a grand grower, has mildew-proof foliage, is startlingly good as a bud, and is exceedingly showy as an overblown bloom, as large as a breakfast saucer." A magnificent bedding rose.

Killarney.—A lovely long well-bred looking pink rose, with beautiful deep bronze-red foliage. It mildews terribly.

Grüss an Teplitz.—A very profuse sweet-scented deep red rose. Very flat and shallow, but fine for cutting and very liberal in growth and bloom. It is practically a pillar rose.

Leonie Lamesch.—The most vivid far-reaching copper-yellow little polyantha rose. It is a glorious bedding variety and unapproachable in colour.

Koenigen Carola.—A great rose, of the softest palest pink, a very strong grower, with a faint sweet scent which puts it in my opinion ahead of Caroline Testout.

Spring Flower Bulbs like Snowdrops, Scillas, Muscari, Chionodoxa, Bluebells, and Crocuses should all be planted in the autumn.

Chionodoxa (Glory of the Snow) is one of our loveliest spring flowers. Its sheets of blue rippling over the rock garden are specially attractive.

The variety Luciliae, with flowers of a brilliant blue with a clear snow-white centre, is deservedly beloved, and the variety Sardensis is one of those rare flowers of a true gentian blue.

Snowdrops (Galanthus) look well in patches of snowy bloom among the turf. All these spring bulbs are friendly accommodating little creatures, and will grow almost anywhere with little cultivation.

Muscari (Grape and Feathery Hyacinth).— The loveliest variety of this is Heavenly Blue, the Starch Hyacinth from Trebizond. The bulbs give a magnificent effect in the garden from April to the end of May, and should be planted with Aubretia, the purple rock cress, especially the variety Dr. Mules, in the rock garden.

Scillas.—Our English bluebell is a Scilla Nutans or Festalis. These little bulbs may be picked up from the woods by those who know where to find them, or bought from the nursery garden and planted in shady places in the autumn. They seed very well, will grow under pines, and go on increasing rapidly.

Sibirica is a very early-blooming spring Bluebell, and this and Bifolia of the Taurus Mountains are well worth massing in the rock garden, and on spring borders.

Lilac I discussed at some length in an early chapter. One of the finest varieties in the garden is Souvenir de L. Spath, which gives a magnificent perfumed bloom of a deep claret colour ; very distinctive and rich. A nice single large white variety is Marie Legraye, and Charles X. a fine reddish-purple.

Guelder Rose (Viburnum Plicatum) will grow in any garden soil ; it is best to plant in the autumn, and it masses well in the spring shrubbery with lilac, hawthorn, laburnum, and syringa.

Red-Hot Pokers are very effective plants for the border. Plants of Tritoma Macowani Dwarf are neat, yielding reddish apricot flowers to a height of one and a half feet.

Tritoma Uvaria Grandiflora. A large variety of the old torch lily or red-hot poker.

Tritoma Yellow Hammer. A clear canary yellow, very distinctive and pretty.

S

Phloxes.—The phlox appears to have originated as a weed in North America, and has come to us through the florists' hands. An exceptionally sturdy comrade in the herbaceous border.

Phloxes are easy plants to grow ; the annuals are raised from seed in spring in the same way as asters. The perennial phloxes can be increased by cuttings or by seed. They thrive in any well drained good garden soil, and yield their best blooms in a wet season. In dry weather they want a good deal of watering.

Good varieties of them are :

Boule de Feu, scarlet.

Lord Raleigh, purple with large heads of flower.

Sylphide, pure white with fine heads of large flowers.

Virginian Creeper can be bought in pots. The ordinary ragged rampant Virginian creeper, apart from Ampelopsis Veitchii, is so common and robust that it seems to me ridiculous to ever buy a plant when one can beg rooted cuttings anywhere and everywhere. The close-clinging Veitchii is more valuable and infinitely more beautiful ; it grows in almost any soil.

Azaleas, in regard to cultivation, I have already mentioned. I do not know the names of any of the varieties. I know that I got my plants after a morning spent walking through some nursery gardens and choosing the colours I liked best, while the plants were in bloom. The foreman tied labels on them, and months later the plants were sent to me for my garden, where they bloom robustly, and increase in stature year by year. I think that probably the most interesting way of choosing the exquisite shades of azaleas to colour, is to do what I did, and go and choose them in the nurseries in bloom.

Pæonies love deep fertile soil and are better protected from the east wind. The best time to plant them is about February or March, but they can be put in any time between October and April. Single plants spread tremendously, though they take a long time to establish. They can be grown from seed, but the better plan is to buy well rooted specimens ; much time is saved that way, and one is sure of getting the varieties that one favours. Some of the modern varieties are extremely beautiful. The name of Kelway of Langport has become indissolubly connected with pæonies ; he specialises in every variety, herbaceous and tree. Perhaps no flower in modern days has been so subject to the hybridist's art, or so generous in the rewards it has yielded. Pæonies have a magnificent perfume and are rivals of the rose and the orchid for sweetness of scent and colouring. They may be naturalised in woodlands, used extensively in the herbaceous border, and indeed would justify any enthusiast in giving them a garden to themselves like roses. The new varieties are very expensive.

The Flag of Truce is the magnificent single white herbaceous pæony; Mafeking a deep blood-red single with a crown of golden anthers.

Princess Duleep Singh is an exceedingly lovely pink.

Queen Alexandra is a most lovely flower of absolute purity of colouring, like an open water lily; faultless white petals of perfect form and great size, with a golden heart.

A very fine line is Kelway's new Imperial

pæonies ; these possess a very distinct style of beauty from any pæonies previously offered to the public. None of them are double as the term has hitherto been applied to pæonies, and yet but a few are perfectly single. All have stout, shell-like guard petals of varying size and form, forming in some a goblet filled to the brim with golden, or rosy, or cream, or white, or particoloured narrow petaloids lying in neat rosette formation ; or with silk-floss-like golden filaments tossing in lovely disorder. The colours are in every case most charming ; they are all of exceptional purity and freshness, including pinks and corals, which are very rare even amongst the choicest of the well-known kinds of former date, and including nothing approaching dull or unpleasing magenta tints. Some of the white varieties are so stout of petal and pure in hue as to remind one of rare water-lilies. Apart from the flowers the foliage has a character distinctive enough to separate them from other kinds. They are just as hardy and require the same treatment as other herbaceous pæonies.

Some of the finest of the imperials are :

King of England; Eileen Kelway, white and salmon.

Another is Thistle, rich blood-crimson with an extraordinary picturesque mass of golden petaloids in the centre.

Plants of the family *Clematis* are not very tiresome about soil, but extremely tricky in the matter of pruning. Clematis Montana, a small spring-blooming white variety, blooms on the young wood and should be pruned in the autumn, leaving all the fresh shoots for next spring's blooming. Clematis Jackmanii and its varieties should be cut down to a bud near the ground every spring. It will grow rampantly from the bud, and soon cover any arch. The more severely the Jackmanii variety of clematis is pruned, the better the blooms and the freer the growth.

Of the Lanuginosa clematis, Venus Victrix, the lavender, is best known. It needs no pruning after planting out. The Viticella type of clematis should be cut back hard every autumn. The only way to be sure about pruning one's clematis plants is to remember the family to which they belong, and make

notes of the habits of each. Directly I know
I have a Jackmanii type of clematis in the
garden, I remember that every February or
March I shall go round and cut mercilessly
back to a good bud near the ground. The
Montana, as I have said in a previous chapter,
I have learned by experience to leave alone.
Of the Lanuginosa varieties I have never
succeeded in raising a decent plant, so I cannot
practice pruning ! These flowers like a nice
deep fibrous loam to root in.

Mignonette and *Love-in-a-Mist* grow best
on chalky soil. They are annuals and may
be sown from packets of seed.

Geraniums are purely bedding plants unless
one has a greenhouse ; there is little to be said
about their culture. I go to the nursery early
in every summer to choose the colour that
will fulfil the purpose of whatever scheme they
are designed for. They like well drained
and fairly light soil.

Crown Imperial (Fritillaria Imperialis) is a
stately hardy border-plant, very effective
in spring when grouped in woodlands, wild
gardens, orchards, etc. Its tall, stout, leafy
stem terminates in a cluster of large drooping

bell-shaped flowers, surmounted by a whorl of fresh green leaves. For forming bold groups in the permanent border or on lawns it is of great value, and should be allowed to remain undisturbed in a good deep loam, planted about five inches deep on their sides, to prevent moisture accumulating in the centre. It is a bulb which requires to become established, and has all the virtues of that fault in the way it blooms year after year without any more trouble. Bulbs should be planted in September.

Gladioli.—Gladiolus bulbs may be had in countless colourings. The July flowering section of gladioli should be planted in spring and produce magnificent spikes of flowers from August till the time of frosts. The section Gandavensis, as also the section Brenchleyensis are the best-known July flowering families. The Colvillei bulbs may be planted in autumn and winter, and are better protected in severe frosts with long straw litter, or some light material. The bulbs of gladioli should by rights be called " corms," though, as I have already said, for practical purposes any distinction is pedantic. Before planting the corms the top soil should be removed and the sub-soil broken up, with a fine dressing of decayed manure dug in. In very light soil constant soaking is necessary. I have already referred to the necessity of lifting the corms after flowering.

Lilies are a very big family, and I have already detailed at some length their necessary culture.

A new lily is Lilium Henryii, the hardy orange-yellow speciosum. It grows well in England in a light sandy soil, and attains a height of six feet or more when established, is very free-flowering, sweet scented, and invaluable for decorations, and should be frequently manured, as it is a very gross feeder. I have never seen it while in bloom, it is still on probation in my garden, but I am pleased to remember that it is likely to be blooming this summer. It was discovered by Dr. Henry in Central China.

Lilium Brownii is a very beautiful lily, producing, in July, handsome trumpet-shaped flowers nearly ten inches long, the tips of the petals reflexing slightly, pure white inside with brown anthers, outside chocolate brown.

It grows to a height of three feet, and does very well in my sandy soil among the azaleas.

Lilium Giganteum (from the Himalayas), is the most majestic of lilies, having stems ten to twelve feet high, when established, with large handsome heart-shaped leaves, and from July to August immense long white trumpet-shaped flowers. Groups of this noble lily in large herbaceous and shrubbery borders, woodlands, or wild gardens, produce a grand effect. They should be planted in a half-shady position, where they can establish themselves and where the subsoil is fairly moist. The large flowering bulbs should be potted up and plunged in a cold frame and then be planted out in May, slight protection from early morning frosts being given. If foliage is made late in the season, after flowering, it must be protected during the winter with straw. The smaller bulbs are specially recommended for naturalising, and will bloom freely two or three years after planting.

Daffodils.—I have used only the name "daffodils," but that name comprises manifold varieties : all the jonquils and narcissi, never forgetting the dear old "pheasant's-eye," the " hoop petticoat " daffodils, " codlins and cream," and Tazetta hybrids, cyclamineus, and all the rest of them. Here are some good garden varieties :

Emperor.—A large handsome golden trumpet, growing about twenty-one inches high, flowering early in April ; splendid for growing and cutting. Good to group for succession with the two following : Henry Irving and Golden Spur, two early favourites, blooming from early March, and growing to eighteen inches.

King Alfred.—A giant trumpet of great beauty and substance, March flowering, height twenty-four inches. A very vigorous grower and free bloomer.

Bernadino.—A grand large pale creamy flower, the cup heavily stained deep orange-apricot.

The Snow-white Daffodil of Spain (Moschatus of Haworth) is an early March bloomer, and cheap withal ; but then it is a dwarf for the rockery or grassy slopes facing north. It is very partial to a certain amount of shade.

Queen of Spain.—An exquisite Triandus hybrid, very pale, very graceful, twelve inches in height, blooming in mid-season and having petals curved back from the trumpet like a cyclamen.

Narcissus Poeticus Recurvus (" Old Pheasant's-Eye ").—One needs not to describe this beloved flower of the spring. Thank the fates it is cheap, and none of us need be without fragrant sheets of it if we wish for them.

Codlins and Cream.—The fat round yellow and white jolly-faced things ! We all know them, I think, with their heavy, overpoweringly sweet scent. They make a noble outcry in April.

Hoop Petticoat.—On the rockery is a pocketful of these queer little trollops in their crinolines. They dance over a carpet of close green, and thrive most happily in sandy peat.

It was such a revelation to me to learn that there were any differences in daffodils that I have dwelled on them at some length in the hope that others may also become interested in their varieties.

PRICES.

HERE are the approximate prices of most of the plants and bulbs mentioned. Any seedsman's catalogue will serve better, as they alter yearly; but I know from my own experience how refreshing it is to get an *idea* of what the plants one would like to have are going to cost. When I first went buying roses I thought they (being so beautiful) must surely cost 7/6 or 10/6 each at the very least. And when I first went buying bulbs I thought a dozen was a lot to buy. It took me months of vainglorious anticipation and a very disillusioned spring to learn that, generally speaking, bulbs want buying by the hundred.

Pansies. Packets of seed from 1d. to 1/-. Plants anything from 3d. to 2/6 each, according to variety.

Tree Lupin from 3d. to 9d. a pot-plant,

which may be planted out any time. It grows readily from seed.

Dwarf Bearded Crimean Irises, 10/6 a hundred or 2/- a dozen. A hundred makes a very fine show indeed. Varieties to name cost more. Pumila Coerulea, for instance, is 5d. a plant, 4/6 a dozen, 27/6 a hundred. Olbiensis Socrates the same. Count Andrassy a trifle less, 4d. each, 3/6 a dozen, 25/- a hundred, and so on. There are over fifty varieties to choose from.

Iris Unguicularis (*Stylosa*) costs 6d. a plant, 5/6 a dozen.

Iris Alata, 15/- a hundred strong selected bulbs, 2/3 a dozen, or 3d. each.

Spanish Irises cost about 1/3 to 2/- a hundred mixed, and anything from 1/6 to 15/- a hundred for named varieties.

English Irises are dearer, generally running about 4/6 a hundred mixed, and 12/6 a hundred named sorts.

Rhododendrons. I have bought small plants of Rhododendron Ponticum for 4d. each, but decent bushy flowering plants cost anything from 18/- a dozen. For the finer varieties in pots one may give anything from 3/- to £30 each.

Pinks cost from 2/- to 3/6 a dozen plants, according to size.

Herbaceous Lupins, Forget-me-nots, Fox-gloves, Wallflowers, Hollyhocks, Sweet Williams, Canterbury Bells, Snapdragons, Columbines, cost 1d. to 6d., packets of seed.

Broom plants in pots, 6d. to 1/- each ; seeds about 1/- a packet.

Tulips from 9d. a dozen to 30/-. The range is immense, 2/- a hundred to £10 a hundred.

Heleniums cost anything from 6d. to 1/- each plant.

Montbretia bulbs cost 5d. a dozen, and 2/9 a hundred to 1/6 each, or 15/- a dozen, according to varieties chosen.

Stocks, 3d., 6d., 1/- or 2/6 packets of seed. Boxes of young plants about 2/6.

Lobelia boxes of well grown plants, 1/6 to 3/6 a box.

Roses can be had from 3d. to 10/6 a plant. The average price is 9d. or 1/- per bush, plants from the open ground, and 1/- to 2/6 for pot plants raised under glass and hardened to the open.

Chionodoxa Luciliae, 4/6 a hundred bulbs, 8d. a dozen.

Chionodoxa Sardensis, 4/- a hund., 7d. a doz.

Crocuses from 1/6 to 3/- a hundred.

Snowdrops (Galanthus) single 2/6 a hundred, double 4/- a hundred, and 5d. and 7d. a dozen respectively.

Muscari, 4/6 a hundred, 8d. a dozen bulbs.

Scilla Nutans bluebells, 3/- a hundred.

Scilla Sibirica about the same.

Lilac, 1/6 a plant or 3/6 a pot plant in named varieties.

Guelder Rose, about 1/6 a plant.

Red-Hot Pokers, 6d. each, 5/6 a dozen for common varieties.

Phloxes, 3d., 6d., and 1/- a plant.

Virginian creeper, about 1/6 a pot plant.

Azaleas, about 2/6 to 3/6 a plant.

Pæonies cost about 10/6 to a guinea each, in the finest new varieties, but strong plants can be had from 3/6 each and less in older varieties.

Clematis from 1/- to 2/6 a pot plant.

Geraniums, anything from 4/- to 30/- a dozen pot plants.

Crown Imperial from 5d. to 1/9 a bulb.

Gladioli cost anything from a guinea a bulb to 8/- a hundred, or less.

Lilies. Candidum, the Madonna lily, cost about 2/6 a dozen.

Lilium Auratum about 5/- to 15/6 a dozen.

Lilium Henryii about 3/6 to 7/6 a bulb.

Lilium Croceum 5/6 a dozen bulbs.

Lilium Brownii 1/- to 2/9 a bulb.

Lilium Giganteum 1/6 to 2/6 a bulb, 15/- to 24/- a dozen, very large selected bulbs.

Daffodils. Emperor, 1/- a dozen to 7/6 a hundred ; Henry Irving and Golden Spur, 8/6 a hundred, 1/3 a dozen; King Alfred, 6/6 a bulb, 3 guineas a dozen; Bernadino, £3 10s. a bulb.

The Snow White Daffodil of Spain, 1/6 a dozen, 2d. each, 10/6 a hundred.

Queen of Spain, 2/6 a dozen, 3d. each.

Narcissus Poeticus Recurvus (Old Pheasant's-Eye) bulbs for naturalising in woods and orchards and on banks and grassy slopes are 1/10 a hundred, 3d. a dozen. Strong garden bulbs are 2/9 a hundred, or 5d. a dozen.

Codlins and Cream, 1/6 a dozen.

Hoop Petticoat Daffodils, from 1/- to 2/- a dozen.

T

INDEX

i